This book is dedicated to my sisters, Michele & Lorraine and to my wife, Helen.

Throughout my life my sisters have always given me love, trust, faith, support and respect. My wife is exactly the same and this is why I love her so much and she is my soulmate.

Thank you from the bottom of my heart to these three amazing ladies, for making me always feel loved and wanted.

My life is special and wonderful by sharing it with you xxx

Chapter 1
An Introduction

My family, friends and people who know me well, will all agree on one very obvious point about me. I love to talk (I do listen no matter what many may say ha ha). I love to make people smile and laugh. Basically I love to make myself feel good and happy.

I believe one of the best sounds you can hear is that of laughter. It is wonderful being with people with everyone laughing and feeling relaxed and happy. I know this is true as I love laughing from a funny comment or hearing a joke or watching hilarious comedy situations on the TV. When I smile, just like other people, it makes me feel good inside and look happy on the outside.

Feeling good inside and out is a win-win situation, something we all want to feel everyday. When I talk and make people laugh, with whatever I have said, I feel good and so do the people around me. So many times people make comments like:- "your sense of humour is amazing" or "where do you come up with all these jokes and one liners?" I have to be honest, it is more in the spur of the moment but I am very quick witted, with a great sense of humour. This is why so many people say they wish they could always be so happy and go lucky just like me and ask me how I do that all the time.

Well the simple truth is although I wish I was like that all the time, it is not possible to be happy every moment of every day. Due to numerous factors that impact us we have many emotions, positive and negative, that alter our behaviour and attitudes and feelings in daily life.

BEHIND THE SMILE people believe you are always happy.

BEHIND THE SMILE surely you have no problems or sadness and you always come over so confident and relaxed. But the simple truth is that for most of the time:-

BEHIND THE SMILE it is not always happy inside for some people including myself. Sadly sometimes we all cover up our true feelings and problems, making us seem we are happy and carefree, however, we know differently.

WE ARE OUR BODY, OUR BODY IS US, RESPECT OURSELVES

Basically, we have to love, respect and care for our body, so we can understand ourselves and love the great gift of life.

BEHIND THE SMILE is written not only for people who have suffered or for anyone who is suffering from any form of depression. It is also designed to be a guide for family, friends and supporters of a person with depression. Allowing those people who have never experienced stages of depression an insight and understanding of how others may be feeling when coping with depression. If family, friends or supporters have had experiences with depression then they themselves will agree on how important love and support are in helping a person who is suffering with depression. Respect and support will help to guide the person back onto the path of health and happiness.

I honestly believe that once you have read this book, you will look at yourself and your life in a completely different and much more positive and confident way.

Yes - you really will….

One thing that every person in the whole world has in common is that we are all HUMAN BEINGS.

Therefore we have to understand that depression can affect any of us because we are all in essence the same.

Depression doesn't just affect a certain type of person. Depression can affect any of us. Anyone can suffer from some degree of depression during their lifetime. It does not matter what sex you are, it doesn't matter what country you were born in. It does not matter what your religion is. It doesn't matter if you are a non-believer. Whatever you age, skin tone, body shape, intelligence, wealth or background. Whether you are a single person or in a relationship or married. It does not matter if you are royalty, a politician, a celebrity or a famous sportsperson. Neither does it matter if you consider yourself to be just an ordinary person. Whatever your career situation, armed forces, NHS worker, student, teacher, retired or a person with a criminal record serving time in a prison, or unemployed, every single person can suffer from depression.

Whatever category you may fall into this may have influences that contribute to your wellbeing and emotional feelings. So we can all be vulnerable suffering from depression. Again no matter how different or similar we are with some of the groups above, we are all human beings.

Basically, we have lots in common. Let's support ourselves, help ourselves and others. You will discover that we can have a wonderful, fulfilling life, happy inside and out. Accept any support that helps you achieve what you deserve, a happy, healthy, fun, rewarding life.

YOU ARE WORTH IT!!

I AM LIKE A FIGHTER ON THE CANVAS

I AM DOWN BUT NOT BEATEN

I WILL FIND THE STRENGTH INSIDE

TO STAND UP AND BEAT THIS ENEMY!

I will admit that having suffered with stages of depression I have learnt to accept that it may occur many times more throughout my lifetime. Although I cannot change this, I can overcome the feelings and endeavour to remain happy, confident, healthy and positive.

At first many of us may not be aware that we have depression. We may not be aware of the signs to inform us. But it may be that we are aware but we prefer to be in denial. This is because sadly the stigma that is attached to depression can influence people not to admit that they have it or that stigma can stop them seeking any form of help.

Denial means that the person may not be able to accept they have the symptoms such as feeling unloved, tearful, empty and withdrawn. Instead they would have themselves believe that they are just tired or overworked for example. This may be a genuine reason in some cases but moreover these symptoms can be a sign of depression. Denial can be easier than admitting something that many feel carries a stigma of a person who you cannot help. Outsiders may see a person with depression as lifeless, boring or even lazy and a person who cannot focus or be bothered to interact. This, of course, is completely incorrect.

No one should feel ashamed or embarrassed by what their body is going through. This may be easier said than done but acceptance is the first stage of beating this unwanted condition. Once you are able to accept you have depression, then help can be found and the process to find a resolution to reduce and control this illness can begin. However long it may take you to find the best treatment suitable for you as an individual, it will be worth it.

It may not be easy but you have been honest with yourself, and you can start to believe that you will be able to control and beat this awful condition for yourself. You have completed the hardest task already, that of acceptance, so well done and you can now start to be positive and work towards achieving what you deserve, a happy and well balanced life.

This is my personal opinion and shared by many others that I have spoken to that have experienced the different stages of depression. The words "mental health" sound very degrading, hurtful and offensive. This is another reason why people find it hard to talk about their feelings as they do not want to be labeled with the stigma of having "mental health issues"

Mental Health is a powerful label and whilst this is known worldwide for medical brain conditions it is still very much off putting for many. Maybe a less harsh or less insulting terminology for example "brain conditions" may help people. After all, it is the brain that controls our thoughts and our emotions. My rant is now over and I stand by my feelings of preferring the term "brain conditions".

Moving on, as I have stated, acceptance is the first stage of dealing with any form of depression. That said I shall accept that the world will continue to use the phrase "mental health" but know whatever label this illness is given, you are special enough and strong enough to accept and control your unwanted condition. I believe in you…………..

Some people will deny how they are feeling and may see no reason to seek help in any form. This is of course their own personal choice. These people may also not appreciate a family member or friend saying that they believe they have a depressive medical condition and again this is their prerogative.

Deep down if we all look at our lifestyles and feelings, they are a true indication of our state of mind, health and wellbeing. I truly know this as I have previously felt ashamed and scared to tell anyone my true low self esteem feelings, during my bleak stages of depression.

I am very fortunate to have a loving family and amazing friends. However, that said, I did not want to tell them my problems and emotional feelings for many reasons. When I was on a low, I felt that I was worthless, a failure and absolutely useless to anyone. Behind the smile, I was fooling others and myself that everything was okay. I was putting on my happy face, fun loving attitude to fool others, as well as myself, that nothing was wrong. This was a complete mistake. My reasoning, at the time, for not telling my loved ones my true feelings was that I did not want to upset them or have them worry about me. I love them too much to hurt them. Eventually, I realised I had in fact hurt them by not telling them. I understand now that they would have helped and supported me from the start and would have made my journey so much easier if only I had been honest with myself and brave enough to tell them.

I could no longer exist, in self pity, feeling worthless and feeling like a failure. I knew denying my feelings was negative and was harming my wellbeing. I spent many hours looking at photographs of my loved ones, walking in the countryside and telling myself these feelings had to be stopped. I told myself to accept that I was suffering from depression and to be strong and to focus on being positive and happy and fun once again.

My main motivation was my sons and other family members, who I love so very much, and I wanted more than ever to overcome the feelings and return to being happy, confident, healthy and positive.

I told myself

One life - live it

I took actions and realised:-

Depression
Is
Acceptable
Is
Controllable
And
Depression
Can Be Beaten!

I BEAT IT!

I was very fortunate to have the love and support of my loving family and friends. It is a difficult and personal decision to confide in anyone and depends on the strength of your relationship with them. Family and friends will always help you, you just need to ask and let them know your true feelings and wellbeing. If at the present time you do not feel able to open up to anyone just take your time until you feel more confident to tell them how you are feeling.

In the meantime, build your courage slowly. Two different approaches to help you to talk and accept how you are feeling so you can approach your family and friends with more confidence are the following:-

Firstly, it may sound strange to some people yet I know many people including myself find this very helpful. Sadly, we have all had loved ones who have passed away. Many people talk to their passed ones on a regular basis for various reasons. By visiting their resting place, we can truly open up our feelings and wishes to them. This way you can find you can be true to yourself having the belief you will be heard. You can tell these people everything and you can assure yourself that there is a positive and healthy future ahead of you. You do not have to just visit your loved ones with sad news but you can go with news when you are feeling more positive and content. This is truly a positive way forward and by opening up to your loved ones who are no longer with us you can now begin to consider approaching your family and friends or seeking professional help.

Secondly, a further simple exercise which provides great help is just to simply fuss with your cat or dog (or a friend or neighbours if you do not have your own). Just by simply stroking any animal your heart beat will slow down and relax you. You can confess your feelings knowing that they will not judge you or answer back. In their own way animals will show their appreciation.

If you have chosen either of these suggestions they will be able to help you open up about your feelings. If you do not wish to try either I have faith in you that you do not want to feel depressed. So please talk to someone and you will receive support and in time will overcome depression. Chapter 10 contains a list of support groups who will listen, care, advise and support you. They will not argue, criticise or judge your situation.

At this stage you will have been honest with yourself that you have depression, now for the next step "Help". If you feel you cannot open up to your family and friends, in addition to the support groups mentioned in Chapter 10 you still have other options that will be able to help you manage and overcome your emotions.

For example, you can make an appointment with your GP. These are highly intelligent, professional medical people who can recommend advice or suggest treatment that may be of great benefit to you. Your GP may diagnose your actual condition for example, mild depression, bi-polar, bereavement, or post natal depression as a few examples. The GP may prescribe you a short course of medication to help you, normally antidepressants. This medication will have the effect of making you feel relaxed and calmer to take life slower and to assist in reducing your depressive feelings. You do not have to take the medication, however, if you decline the medical advice provided by your GP, you must inform them. It may be wise to have a follow up appointment with your GP to see if you are managing to cope with or without the prescribed medication. You will probably find your GP will give you advice that will be able to help you, so please respect their knowledge, judgement and help.

As you will read about later in this book, the GP may recommend a form of counselling which may include CBT (cognitive behavioural therapy). The GP may also advise a healthy diet, regular exercise and a good sleep pattern.

Your GP may also give you details of a local support group. A counsellor will show you empathy, to understand your feelings and views without judging you. Maybe you will feel comfortable talking to a teacher, a works manager, a vicar or person of your faith. Whomever you choose they will be able to help you in some positive form. Go with an open, positive mind and be honest that you need support with your feelings and let yourself receive the support they provide. If you find you have not found enough help to deal with your feelings, persevere and do not be too hard on yourself and you will control your condition by eventually finding a source of help that suits you and your circumstances.

You may wish to try some alternative therapies (further details are contained within Chapter 7).

Alternative therapies are my personal favourites and I am convinced that people who have depression or those without depression will benefit greatly from this type of therapy.

When I stopped being in denial and accepted that I had depression I did not feel like a failure anymore I felt truly relieved like a great weight had been lifted off my shoulders. It was time for me to accept my illness and to focus on each day as it came and to give myself realistic targets to focus on so I could achieve them and I DID!!!!

Life Is For Living

Love Is For Giving and Receiving

With the support of my family and friends and my chosen alternative therapies I have controlled and beaten my old enemy depression. I accept that due to situations that I cannot control I shall be challenged again throughout my lifetime.

I can honestly say that I still do on occasions have depressive feelings but my knowledge and experience means that I can now control these feelings. My method to overcome these depressive feelings is to cry my eyes out and let these negative feelings take over my body for a short period of time. By then I know my mind and body will be in a stronger place and I shall accept what caused this feeling. I will be stronger and more positive as I appreciate that life is special and worth living. I love the sound of laughter and I hate the sadness of crying. So like myself, you can be strong and beat depression. Retrain your brain, love life and love yourself and others. We can all be truly happy BEHIND THE SMILE and really feel and mean it.

Chapter 2
Depression, Stress and Anxiety

Apart from depression, sadly there are two other major similar health conditions which are stress and anxiety.

Some people may never suffer from these conditions. Although for the vast majority of people one of these conditions, maybe two or even three of them will affect them at some point during their lifetime.

There can be many different reasons, for example, due to our lifestyles, daily demands, emotional pressures and our home environments to name just a few examples.

Although depression, stress and anxiety cause our bodies to have different physical and emotional feelings when suffering from any of these conditions the symptoms can be very similar to each other.

Sadly suffering from depression, stress and anxiety makes the individual feel physically and emotionally different to how a person with no symptoms would be feeling. However, all three conditions can be controlled and managed by understanding the situation and our bodies better, therefore all three conditions can be beaten.

When the sufferer feels strong enough to open up and ask for help, that is a huge achievement and needs to be respected. Whatever reasons or situations are causing a person to suffer from depression, stress or anxiety you have to show them that you really want to help them on their road to a happy and fun loving life.

For the person offering that all important support to the person suffering from depression, stress and anxiety:-

IF THEY TALK - LISTEN.....

Always try to understand and respect them. Please never say "pull yourself together" or "it is not that bad" or a similar type of phrase, as this is likely to stop them from asking for the help that they may need and will make them feel that nobody believes that their feelings are genuine or that anyone wishes to help them. Please refrain from using the words "you do not know how lucky you are" as they will not be feeling lucky and are suffering and trying to find the happy life they deserve again.

If you are a family member or a loved one, friend or a kind hearted supporter trying to help the individual I would like to personally thank you for showing the love and kindness and respect to whomever you are helping. The individual will also really appreciate your time and effort with them even if they do not tell you at the moment in time they will.

For the person suffering with this illness, I have faith that your wellbeing shall improve, by reading this book. You will control your condition better and become a happier, healthier person and will believe in your wonderful self. Therefore, whatever form of support you chose, please smile and thank whomever it is that helps you.

Every day we are placed in different situations that require us to make decisions and take the necessary actions.

However, when we do not feel strong enough or believe enough in ourselves we can become emotional and depression, stress or anxiety can take over our wellbeing.

Being faced with unwanted confrontations and problems on a regular basis does change how we feel and behave. We may become nervous, scared, feel under pressure or even angry. How we can control this is down to the actions we take. Different people act differently in different situations. For example some people keep their emotions bottled up and others explode with anger. Whatever your behaviour trait is it would be much nicer to be able to resolve certain unwanted feelings to situations in a calmer relaxed way for ourselves and others.

Depression, stress and anxiety share both similar and different symptoms to each other. By recognising these symptoms, feelings, signs and behavioural patterns you should be able to determine what you are suffering from and look for ways to help you control your symptoms. Whatever your background, age or other categories you put yourself in as we all know we are all human beings, this should mean that not only should we help ourselves and help others it also means that we should never suffer alone.

Look into my eyes
I really need a friend
I need help with my feelings
I can no longer pretend

Some symptoms of Depression are

- Low self esteem
- Sadness
- Loneliness
- A feeling of worthless
- Tearful
- Lost of interest in family, friends and hobbies
- Lack of motivation

Some symptoms of Stress are

- Anger
- Feeling overwhelmed
- Being moody
- Quick tempered
- Exhaustion

Some symptoms of Anxiety are

- Fear
- Tense
- Nervous
- Restless
- Worry with or without actual reasons
- Panic attacks

Some shared symptoms of all three conditions are

- Fatigue
- Problems sleeping
- Raised blood pressure
- Headaches
- Being irritable
- Change in appetite

Depression will be explained in more detail later in this book. However, there is medical evidence that shows depression, stress and anxiety can take the person suffering from one condition to another.

Stress is seen as a physical or emotional change that can be controlled once the problem has gone away. Severe stress can lead to anxiety. Being anxious can mean that the individual is always worrying about what might or may not happen. Severe anxiety can lead to depression.

The term "fight or flight" is when the body releases chemicals known as adrenaline, noradrenaline and cortisol when we are faced with a stressful or frightening situation. Your heart beats quicker and blood pressure greatly increases, breathing can become deeper and taking in more oxygen and muscles tense. Our brain makes the quick decision to fight or flight (stay or run) from the pending situation.

Mild stress or anxiety in limited amounts can be good for you. This may sound strange but this is because when our bodies are faced with stress or anxiety it can motivate us to solve the problem or tasks and keep us alert and focussed. If we can manage our stress and anxiety then this will not harm our daily wellbeing. But, if both of these conditions are not controlled or treated this can lead to developing stages of depression.

This is also true of suffering from depression. When we are at a low, finding life difficult to cope with. We may become stressed or anxious with life, family and work. Before explaining stress and anxiety a little more please do not lose hope of controlling any of these three unwanted conditions.

Help is available in various forms especially if you go in "open minded" and you really want to help yourself. However, daily life will always challenge us with unforeseen circumstances.

Stress

Stress is an unpleasant and challenging feeling giving an unwanted change to our bodies physical and emotional daily wellbeing. Everyday we can face difficult choices and situations. The situations can cover many categories from family relationships, financial worries, health issues, education, working environment and literally anything that can give us reason to make us act and behave differently.

Stress is a symptom that unless dealt with and controlled can spiral into very unhealthy medical conditions which we really need to try and avoid. Whether or not you are in education, employment, or non-working, we all tend to follow daily routines. We never know exactly what will happen each and every day but generally we have a good idea. We are normally prepared and go about our usual routine, however, we can never be prepared for the unexpected events that may suddenly happen in our daily lives.

If you are in education, stress is definitely one thing you can do without. Sadly you may encounter it more times than you would like but hopefully a solution will be able to help you control the experiences of stress. Within all education establishments there are challenges and demands expected from all students. Circumstances such as coursework, home life problems, bullying or relationships have a bearing on how our bodies cope with stress.

That said when put in unwanted situations such as a teacher or lecturer belittling students or not helping explain work even giving far too much work for them to cope with the body sends out warning signs. By feeling under pressure maybe becoming angry and verbal our bodies react to the circumstances of the issues and confrontation.

I would just like to say I am using a teacher or lecturer as an example. I know they do wonderful jobs and only have their students' best interests and education at heart. The teacher or lecturer is also likely to suffer, at some time, from depression, stress or anxiety due to their very demanding career choice.

Stress is also very common in most workplaces. There can be many different reasons why we can become stressed at work; these can range from various issues with management, colleagues or customers. Not only in education or work can an individual experience unwanted stressful situations, just in everyday life we can be challenged by unpleasant events.

There are numerous situations which occur in our day to day lives and any one of these can bring on stress.

There are many stress symptoms which include but are not inclusive of a raised blood pressure, a faster heart beat, feeling overwhelmed, frustrated, nervous, angry and even at times violent.

For your own wellbeing the outcome needs to help you calm down and unwind. When in stressful situations you really need to try and stay as calm as possible. Take slow deep breaths to relax you, step back and re-evaluate the situation. Eventually, once the issue has been resolved your stressful feelings will stop.

It is very important for your wellbeing to control your actions and behaviour when stressed. You really should see your GP or contact a support group (see chapter 10) as stress is very serious and harmful to your health.

There can be three stages of stress that the body may experience. The first stage is known as the "alarm stage". This is when the body first becomes aware of a threat, creating fear and uncertainty which leads the body to create the fight or flight situation. Do you stay and deal with the situation or do you avoid it and leave? The choice is down to the individual and the situation. It may be best to stay this time and sort the unwanted situation out calmly or maybe if you feel at this time the outcome would not be what you would like then you can calmly turn away and avoid the confrontation until an appropriate moment will allow you and the other party to agree on an acceptable solution.

The second stage is known as the "resistance stage". This is when the body uses the nervous system to try and control the heart rate by lowering to a more normal beat. By lowering the heart beat and blood pressure our minds can focus more clearly and concentration will improve.

If you find yourself in regular situations of stress this would be known as the third stage which is called the "exhaustion stage". This is when your body is really struggling to work at its best to maintain your wellbeing. If you are stressed for a long period your immune system weakens. You will become physically and psychologically drained and tired. Also becoming more irritable and unable to eat and sleep properly, this is your body telling you to take a break. You will need to try and step back and unwind and put yourself and your health first. If you do not, a very serious unwanted health condition could follow.

None of us like to be unwell and restricted from doing all the lovely things that we are able to enjoy. However, for many different reasons our health conditions can exclude us from a daily fun and healthy lifestyle. Therefore you have to discover ways to help you overcome what you are suffering from, in this instance, it is stress. Firstly, you have to admit that you are suffering from stress and its symptoms. Not only may it be harming your health but also the health of family, friends and others around you. So you admit you have a problem, the next important stage is how to deal with it, initially finding the cause. Stress can be caused by a number of reasons for example, money worries, relationship problems, school, education or working environment or a situation where you could suddenly erupt in anger and rage when confronted by a certain person or situation.

The next stage is handling the cause of the stress. Maybe you could try to chat to those who are making you feel stressed. After all, talking is usually the best way forward to solve a number of situations including stress. Hopefully by chatting to others this will make you more open and create a better working environment with a calmer and friendly atmosphere for all. Becoming more organised in your daily life will assist in making targets easier to achieve be that work targets or just getting dinner on the table for the family.

If you are not confident in discussing these matters then perhaps writing the problems down will give you the confidence to discuss matters. Having a written record of your feelings means that you will be able to see in black and white the situation and it may be that by seeing the words in front of you, it will give you insight into the situation.

It is always very wise and helpful to seek professional advice from your GP. The GP will be able to inform you of ways to control your stress with or without medication.

From my own personal experience I found that alternative therapy and a good diet and regular exercise made all the difference to me. Details of alternative therapies are contained within Chapter 7 and details of diet, exercise and sleep are provided within Chapter 8. Other things I found to help control my stress were thinking positively, practising controlled breathing techniques, listening to calming music and taking leisurely walks.

Anxiety

The three conditions of depression, stress and anxiety are all unwanted health conditions that we do not wish to experience, but sadly almost every person will. The more we understand how our body feels and works the better we can control any of these conditions. It is not unusual to be anxious at times over such matters as money problems, changing school or careers, even medical examinations. However, some people sadly suffer from panic attacks regularly and being nervous which can lead to anxiety.

There are different reasons why an individual will suffer with anxiety. It can be going through stages of extreme stress and events that can be very traumatic. Sadly the events can be very different ranging from physical abuse to emotional abuse even horrific situations such as being a witness to a critical accident or seeing a person attacked will have an unwanted impact on the individual.

Left untreated these episodes will remain with the individual and during life will be harder to deal with and daily tasks could become a challenge and sometimes overwhelming.

Whilst some people may feel that they do not wish to talk about their anxiety, we should all realise we all deserve to live a healthy, wonderful and fulfilling life. Our life is a gift and it is paramount that we enjoy our life and loved ones within it. Our wellbeing is so important, no matter what condition we are suffering from silence is not a help, talking will help deal with the situations and help to improve your wellbeing.

Do not stay silent

Talking helps

Let others help you

Anxiety has four different levels depending on how severe its impact is on an individual's physical and emotional wellbeing.

The first level is known as mild anxiety. This is when the person may have normal feelings of uncertainty about forthcoming events. The events can include examinations, medical appointments, job interviews or even a romantic date. The thought of hoping everything goes well but on the other hand it may not, can cause doubts that the occasion may not go as well as hoped and the individual could experience mild anxiety feelings such as lack of concentration, sweating and shyness.

Level two is known as moderate anxiety. This is when a person will spend most of the day feeling anxious and will panic that they are not able to control events or situations that they are faced with. Their bodies may experience feelings of being on edge and are unable to relax.

Level three is known as severe anxiety. The symptoms become a little more intense at this stage. The person suffering will have anxious feelings all day and will try to avoid situations and people that they feel may affect them. They have a preference to be alone and can experience heart palpitations, chest pain, breathlessness and may find it difficult to concentrate and may experience feelings of fear.

The final stage is level four which is known as panic anxiety. This is a very serious illness as the individual can suffer from panic attacks. This is caused by unwanted overwhelming feelings that everything is going to be a disaster and nothing will work out as it should. The individual will be unable to carry out daily tasks and their body may experience very serious unwanted feelings.

These four levels of anxiety are all unwanted but they are all common in people everywhere. You are not the only suffering person so help is out there, go get it, you deserve it. Whilst stress goes after the event has passed anxiety can continue even after the event has passed. Learning how to control these experiences is very important and simple techniques such as gentle breathing exercise and meditation can be a great way to help you relax. Focus on your own personal achievements that you are proud of to produce positive thoughts that can help you realise life is rewarding and fun.

It is always very wise and helpful to seek professional advice from your GP. The GP will be able to inform you of ways to control your anxiety with or without medication.

Contained within Chapter 10 are details of support groups which can help you deal with depression, stress and anxiety.

Chapter 3
What is depression and its causes?

Depression is a medical condition that affects a person by making them have negative thoughts and feelings about themself and life in general. Depending on the severity of depression the symptoms can vary.

There can be many reasons that can make an individual experience physical and emotional feelings that affect their daily wellbeing. Later in this chapter a selection of examples will be used to explain why some people experience depression. However, for now we will look at the medical side of how the brain is affected by the emotional impact that depression has on our bodies and how our bodies try to control these unwanted negative emotions. The brain is the control centre of our body. Different parts of the brain have different functions and responsibilities to carry out. The three main parts of the brain, located in the limbic system, that control functions relating to feelings such as depression are the amygdala, hippocampus and the thalamus.

The amygdala is mainly associated with the feelings and emotions relating to fear, threats, aggression and happiness. It stores these events that the individual has experienced so in future situations the memories can be retrieved to allow the individual to prepare for those similar situations. For happiness it can be anything very personal or significant to the individual, ranging from winning an award of any kind, getting married or becoming a parent. On the other extreme it also stores memories such as shame and grief.

The amygdala is best known for being responsible for the body's "fight or flight" process. This is when the individual is confronted by a fearful and threatening situation that they were not expecting. It can range from a confrontation at home, work or in another environment. It may be verbal or physical or maybe avoided depending on the individual's response to the handling of the fight or flight situation.

The experience of fight or flight is when suddenly the amygdala sends out emergency panic signals when in a fearful or threatening situation. This makes the body react to the threat of confrontation.

The adrenal glands suddenly release adrenaline into the bloodstream. Blood is directed to major organs, the brain becomes more active, the heart beats faster, blood pressure rises and breathing becomes faster, which also allows the lungs to take in more oxygen. The arms, legs and body muscles receive more blood and oxygen to them to prepare for a threatened attack or reaction. The adrenal glands release cortisol which stimulates the liver to release glucose (sugar), in the stressful time of need for faster energy. The body is on high alert should the individual decide to stay and confront the person (fight) or should they use energy to be safe and avoid confrontation and run away (flight). Whatever the outcome, the body will need to relax and calm down after the event. Deep controlled breathing will help lower the heartbeat and blood pressure. All people and situations are different and are all controlled differently. Depression can affect the individual's mood swings, lack of motivation even feeling tearful.

Your health is always very important
You are very important
Taking care of your health
Is taking care of yourself

The hippocampus is part of the brain mostly responsible for learning and memory. When we study and learn information and facts that our brain considers to be important, the hippocampus then stores this for our long term memories. These memories can range from a variety of events and occasions. Memories can be stored and retrieved from childhood experiences like school friends and birthday parties, memories of holidays and other significant occasions.

The hippocampus also plays a significant role in remembering facts for educational purposes or working life. It also stores what is known as spatial navigation. This is, for example, when a driver goes on a regular route to a particular destination, the memory recalls certain roads, buildings or landmarks the driver has seen previously so as to take the correct route to the destination. The brain needs to stay simulated - healthy mind - healthy body - reading, writing, doing puzzles or watching TV quiz shows are all wonderful ways of learning. Any form of learning knowledge keeps the brain functioning better.

When our body is suffering from a form of depression, this affects the hippocampus. As the hippocampus' main responsibilities are learning and memory depression can cause the individual to find it hard to focus, they can lose concentration, become confused or forgetful. Once depression has been controlled the hippocampus and other regions of the brain can then function correctly.

The thalamus is known as the body's relay station. Its vital function is to receive, process and transmit sensory information received from around the body and send onto the cerebral cortex for final analysis so that the information can be finally processed to carry out the particular function required. This includes how the body moves, to see, hear, taste and touch but does not include smell (that is the olfactory system). The thalamus is also a factor to process and regulate feelings of sexual arousal, along with learning, memories and emotions that we experience. When the individual is suffering different stages of depression the body functions in a different way than when the individual is happy, calm, relaxed and feeling positive about themselves and life. Depending on the stage of depression the feelings can vary from low self esteem, lack of confidence, tiredness, loss of interest in oneself and loss of interest in social interactions.

The body also produces natural hormones to help control our wellbeing. Cortisol is a natural hormone also known as the "stress hormone" created in the body. In the base of the brain is a gland known as the pituitary gland. The pituitary gland receives information and decides if the cortisol levels are well balanced to normal, or if they are low and need to be increased. If they need to be increased signals are sent to the adrenal glands, which are two glands, one located on each kidney. From here cortisol can be produced and released into the bloodstream and travel throughout the body.

Having a controlled level of cortisol helps us control the level of blood pressure. Too much cortisol can lead to high blood pressure where too little cortisol can lead to a low blood pressure. For instance, when the body is faced with a very stressful sudden situation known as fight or flight, cortisol is released to keep the individual alert. Cortisol will cause a release of glucose (sugar) from the liver so that the body can receive energy during this event. Although cortisol is a very important hormone for the body, producing too much by being stressed a lot of the time to high levels, can lead to a negative impact on the individual's wellbeing. A healthy diet, routine exercise and good sleep can help this from developing into eventual depression for individuals.

Dopamine is known as the happy hormone. Dopamine's role within the body is to help with movement, concentration, learning and motivation. When we are experiencing events that give us great pleasure, or feeling of reward such as cuddles with a loved one, massage, lovemaking, singing along to our favourite songs, cardio workouts any of these can give us great pleasure and dopamine gives us a natural high by being released.

If our body does not produce enough dopamine we can have low motivation or lack of concentration leaving us lethargic and uninterested in daily life. This can be caused by the intake of too much junk food, poor sleep and taking prohibited drugs.   To increase levels to a safe, normal, healthy level we should   maintain   the   experiences   that   give   us pleasure.

Serotonin   is   a   hormone   and   very   similar   to dopamine, although both are responsible for giving the   individual   the   happy   or   pleasurable   feeling, serotonin has a longer lasting effect on the events that we enjoy. Nearly all the serotonin is produced in our intestines, with the remainder being produced in the brain. Its function for the body is helping with happiness,   learning,   mood,   emotions,   appetite, digestion, sleep patterns, sexual desire and blood clotting. If levels of serotonin are low the person can suffer from a reduction of its functions. A good way to increase serotonin within the body is by healthy eating, regular exercise, a good sleep schedule and enjoying the outdoors and sunshine.

Endorphins are a natural body hormone. They are produced in the brain by the hypothalamus and pituitary gland. Endorphins can be released when the body is enjoying activities that give it great pleasure. These can range from exercise for example running. Sometimes whilst running a runner may experience a sudden feel good rush known as a runner's high. Endorphins are being released and the runner will experience a short feeling of sensation in their body. Essentially these hormones are released to promote good feelings during activities that we enjoy doing. However, endorphins are not only produced and released during physical activity, our body also releases them as our natural pain killer. This works by endorphins being released to cause blocking to the nerve cells that would receive messages that the body was in pain or muscles ache. Looking after ourselves helps our body function much better and healthily.

What causes depression and to what level of depression varies from person to person and situation to situation. Some people can suffer from the same situations as others, yet cope completely differently. Sadly, if you are struggling with depression and other events happen that you cannot cope with, the severity of depression can increase. This is why it is very important to be honest, strong and brave and talk about your feelings and ask for help. Never be afraid or ashamed because you are never the only person suffering from depression. This is why it is very important to talk to someone about how you are feeling. The more you talk about your feelings the easier it is to find support and work through them. Hopefully you would be able to talk to your family, friends, wellbeing support colleagues, your GP, a counsellor or any of the wonderful support groups in Chapter 10. Depression can cover many emotions and feelings; they can include any of the following: - low self esteem, feeling sad, unloved, unwanted, lonely, worthless, irritable and angry. They can make you suffer from fatigue, sleep problems and changes to appetite. They can even include feeling sensitive, having little or no motivation or loss of interest in family, friends, work, education and socialising and even a loss of interest in hobbies.

You may find it hard to concentrate and have difficulty remembering or staying focused. Basically, depression makes a person self doubt and not believe in themselves. It also makes them feel that love, fun, pleasure, laughter and happy times will never return. Believe me this is not true, they will return. People suffering from depression do not always ask for help as they may feel others do not understand or care. The following events can have a dramatic effect on a person's wellbeing. How we manage to accept and deal with these events decides if we suffer from depression and to what extreme. Please remember you must try to always talk about your feelings of depression. Do not suffer and struggle in silence. This may well have a negative impact on your wellbeing and will increase the severity of your depressive symptoms.

Many situations can cause depression. A breakdown of some of the situations will follow. However, if your situation is not included it is still very important that you find help and support.

Childhood

If at an early age a child experiences an awful event that causes them a trauma or even worse two or more events then there would be a high chance that person could relive and suffer from these awful events causing depression in later life. Examples of such trauma are: -

When a child experiences the death of a family member or someone close to them if the child did not receive comfort and support at the time they can find it extremely difficult to deal with similar circumstances later in life.

The experience of being physically or sexually abused is a life changing experience for any child. The victim should never blame themselves for the awful events that have occurred. These experiences can leave the child finding it hard to trust and love people again.

In childhood even a natural occurrence as bedwetting can distress the sufferer. They can feel ashamed and scared of being teased if people find out. There are different causes for bedwetting, for example, drinking too much prior to bedtime, suffering from nervous feelings or medical reasons such as a urinary tract infection or even having a small bladder can contribute to bedwetting. The longer the sufferer feels ashamed and worries about it without getting advice the longer it will take to sort the problem out and control it.

Any of these traumas will affect the child's emotions from low self esteem, lack of confidence, being tearful, feeling unloved, being withdrawn, feeling frustrated and even feeling angry.

In the first instance a child should try to talk to a family member or someone that they trust. If this is not possible then there are a number of well known support groups who are there to help children of all ages particularly the NSPCC Childline. Full details of these can be found in Chapter 10.

Bereavement

The shock and pain of bereavement can lead to depression. At any age the passing of a loved one or a very special person is heartbreaking and can be very difficult to accept. Any loss is always soul destroying. How you can come to accept death can make all the difference. It is totally natural to be empty, to cry, or even be angry to have lost that special someone. Sometimes people cannot attend the funeral for various reasons. However, some people do not attend the funeral of a loved one as they do not want to accept their death.

On the other hand some people attend the funeral as a way of closure and to start to accept the passing of the deceased. If this natural heartbreaking event has left you feeling that life is not worth living or you will never feel happy again please find support. Never suffer in silence and try to speak to family, friends, your GP, a counsellor, a support group or a person of religious standing or whomever you can turn to for support.

People will understand your sadness and sometimes may not ask how you are feeling because they do not want to upset you or may feel so many other people have asked you the same question. Sometimes people may seem to be asking lots of questions but generally it means that they care about you and feel that talking will help you open up and accept the awful loss a little better.

At this sad time sometimes people do not always say the right thing but they may feel nervous. One question you are most likely to be asked is "how are you coping?. This loss will take its toll on you in many ways but how you cope is very important to your wellbeing. Stay focused, find help and steadily your life, will hopefully, improve again. Certainly, you may always feel a loss and it is never fair for anyone to pass away. You should never feel alone. Find some form of support. There are really plenty of people and support groups ready and able to help you.

Relationships

A major contributor to depression comes when we experience relationship problems. In an ideal world most of us would love to find our soulmate, get married, have children and live happily ever after. Well that would be wonderful but even the greatest of relationships will endure some form of sadness, no matter whatever future we dream of. A wonderful relationship is where we feel loved, secure, happy and enjoy being with our loved ones. This is why when something goes wrong in a relationship we can just fall apart broken hearted. It can be your first love, a break up after a period of time or an engagement called off. You can be married and the marriage breaks down and leads to divorce. A loved one could just walk out and you lose contact with them, leaving you heartbroken and feeling empty. Whatever the situation, unless the break up is mutually agreed the pain of not being with the person you love really can send you into a soul destroying very unwanted lonely place experiencing many negative feelings.

Moreover, if children are involved within the relationship break down it can become very painful for them as well as the parents. It is always very important that the children know that they are loved and wanted by both their parents. A failed relationship can lead to depression where you feel your world has been turned upside down and you feel empty and worthless. Some people will find this harder to cope with than bereavement knowing the loved one is still alive but no longer wants to be with them. Depending on the situation and who is involved, like everything with a problem, talking helps. Do not lock yourself away, you really need to talk to a person who can help you.

Health

Suffering from health problems or a long term illness can have a dramatic effect on a person's wellbeing. From a short term health condition to a lifelong illness these can cause the sufferer symptoms of depression. Under regular visits to GPs and hospitals, along with receiving all the care and medical knowledge and support the individual can still be scared, worried and become depressed.

A person should seek all guidance and reassurance concerning their medical condition from medical professionals which should help alleviate their fears and concerns which will assist in helping suppress the symptoms of depression.

Loneliness

A misconception is that loneliness only happens to the elderly, this is totally untrue.

The feeling of loneliness can affect anyone, who is living alone or not. A person can be living with others, like family, in a relationship or house sharing. It may sound surprising but even having others around the person can feel there is no love, respect, fun, interaction, or conversation to make them feel happy, special, needed, wanted and even noticed.

Different environments and different circumstances can contribute to a person experiencing feelings of loneliness. This can be very common with young people in any level of education. Although surrounded by lots of other students it can still be a very difficult environment to interact and make friends which may lead to loneliness. There can be many reasons for this, these can range from problems in their home life, moving to a new location to live and study where they do not know anyone. Finding it hard to be accepted by some people due to reasons like being naturally shy, their clothing choices, accent, even their sexuality. Sadly, this has always been a difficult time as this is a process of growing up.

For people currently experiencing this do not give up, have faith and you will get through these times and will become a stronger person.

I hope you do discover kind and genuine people that you share a common interest with and become good friends. You may wish to join a club or group, near where you are studying, that you enjoy. Rather than sitting alone, lessons and life become easier with friends and talking about your feelings. There should be forms of counsellors in education establishments that are available for advice and support. Everyone should realise that they are not alone with their feelings and this is why there are support people and counsellors to help.

Sadly, other reasons contribute to loneliness ranging from bad medical news or the passing of a loved one (being human or animal form), it may also be caused by a relationship breakup, all leaving the individual wanting to stay indoors and hide from others and the outside world. Working from home or being elderly, when the front door closes the feelings of being all alone can cause depression.

Ways of improving a person's wellbeing is social interaction. Joining local clubs and groups is a wonderful way to make new friends and these benefit the person's wellbeing in a positive way. If you know someone who is alone you could always visit them or call them to see how they are. People should never feel unwanted or that nobody cares so pick that phone up and phone that friend for a chat.

Retirement

When people decide to take retirement we hope that they will be able to take life at a slower pace and enjoy a well deserved retirement. We hope that they can enjoy any hobbies or interests they have or would like to do.

People who retire usually have more time to spend with family and friends and "their time" to do whatever they always wanted to do but never had the time whilst they were working. Along with these ideas we do hope that they are financially secure once retired.

Unfortunately, retirement for some people is not as special and rewarding as they may have expected. Sadly due to some of the following circumstances that they may encounter they may experience episodes of depression. An individual may not have any hobbies or interests that they enjoy or wish to pursue. Sadly, if they do not have family or friends close by they can find themselves isolated and lonely. By no longer working and without having a reason to get out of bed in the morning and not being able to interact with people they may lose interest in daily life and lose motivation for daily tasks. Whilst working the income will have helped pay the bills and other expenses but that does not always mean that an individual has sufficient savings to live securely once they are no longer earning. Financial worries are a very big problem that greatly causes people to suffer from depression in the same way that loneliness can.

In retirement, the individual can struggle with their wellbeing due to feeling they are no longer wanted or needed like they were whilst working. Retirement can lead to a totally new lifestyle and some people may not adjust as well as others. A retired person should be proud of their working life achievements. A new chapter in their life book can be written.

If you are retired please remember that you have so much knowledge and experience to pass on to others. You could consider joining local sporting or social clubs or community groups to enjoy events and other peoples company. Please enjoy your deserved retirement. Use this opportunity to enjoy exercise for example, walking and swimming and gardening (tea and cake at the garden centre) and the fun of cooking. Life can really be more relaxing, calmer when retired and you really deserve it.

Finance

Due to various reasons the lack of money and ability to pay outgoings and debts, let alone make savings, can contribute to depression for many people.

Credit card debts, mortgage, rent, fuel, clothing and food are just a few of the main financial commitments that we spend our money on. When struggling to pay financial commitment, a lack of money can really have a negative impact on a person's wellbeing and it is totally acceptable that the individual may feel worried and emotional.

It may sound harsh but the following may be the solution to accepting the financial crisis and in turn control the depressive episodes that may arise due to the stress of the financial situation. The person needs to take a step back, take a deep breath and try to focus and reassure themselves that there is a positive solution that can be found. It may be difficult but it would be wise to accept the circumstances and talk to someone about how they are struggling financially. Maybe the individual has some savings that they could use to help them for a short period of time.

Some people may wrongly feel ashamed and/or embarrassed but asking family or friends for a financial loan could be the solution even if only for a short while. Other options are contacting financial professionals for genuine financial advice and guidance.

Maybe some non essential spending can be reduced or stopped to create some extra cash. People should never go without food and water and in the UK many amazing groups, organisations and food banks offer food parcels for people in need. These groups are there for those individuals who are struggling to buy these items. A person should accept the kindness of others to help them through difficult times. When life does improve they can, like many of us, buy a little extra food to assist others in times of hardship.

A very sad situation is when pet owners can no longer afford to feed their pets or take them to the vets for treatment. People in this situation can reach out to animal organisations who can offer advice and support to try and keep owners and pets together for the love and wellbeing of both the owner and the pet.

Guilt

This is a negative emotional feeling that a person can suffer from by keeping the personal behaviour or actions that they have carried out against others bottled up inside them. This can be from circumstances such as lying, theft or criminal action, denying the truth and not taking responsibility for their own actions.

The person suffering with guilt can feel that their actions are totally reasonable. But really they are not if they are making innocent people suffer for events that were not their fault.

Given an opportunity to make things right if the individual does not confess the real truth, sadly they may lose out. Not only does the person making wrongful allegations suffer from guilt which may lead to depression the innocent party will also wrongly suffer and could lose respect, friends, their career and even freedom and may also suffer from depression. Is living with certain lies doing anyone's wellbeing any good? If you are suffering with guilt and depression is affecting your wellbeing and lifestyle it could be a good time to talk to somebody for both yours and others wellbeing.

Moving house

Due to different reasons people move homes. Usually, moving to be nearer relations, or a change of job or lifestyle. This can be a great change in people's lives and not always in a positive way. The move may be essential but the unknown future may feel daunting to some, having a negative effect on their wellbeing. The fear of maybe leaving family and friends behind, can be very difficult, however, it does not mean that people should not stay in regular contact with each other. The person may be surprised and enjoy their new home and its location.

Hopefully, by joining local groups and attending local events, new friendships can be created. However, if the move does unsettle the person and their wellbeing suffers, they really need to talk to family, friends or another form of support so that they can express their feelings and concerns.

Genetic inheritance

On this subject I have chosen not to include statistics and findings on how it may be passed down to family members. You may have family members who have suffered from different stages of depression and it may be known that you have inherited similar symptoms as these family members. Sadly, as we all realise, accepting and dealing with depression can be very difficult. Although it helps when we can discover and admit the real cause of the depression we are experiencing. If a person therefore knows how bad they have been suffering with depression then they should realise how the family member who shares the similar condition is also feeling. Therefore giving support to each other.

Inherited genes are not passed to family members by choice. So together more than ever the family members concerned should help and support each other, not passing blame but focusing on controlling their depression and dealing successfully with it together.

Physical

There are two very soul destroying types of bullying. In no particular order there is physical bullying (using a person's body strength to control and attack another person). The other form is psychological bullying where instead of using physical violence the bully uses psychological (mind games) and verbal abuse to their victim.

Physical Bullying

This is when the bully uses physical force to attack or harm another individual. This can be over a short period of time or over months or even years. It is usually when one person wants to become dominant over another person to get them to do what the bully wants, not what the victim would like to do. Situations can vary from educational bullying where someone decides to physically attack a student or teacher, for any unexcusable reason, maybe to steal money or personal belongings, maybe as they are getting higher grades than the bully, they are of different sexual orientation and have different religious beliefs. Being physically attacked for any reason is very frightening and unacceptable.

Furthermore, to actually witness it and record it on a mobile (unless you wish to use it as evidence against the bully) is unacceptable. If you are a person who records such an event, then releases it on social media you are almost as bad as the bully. Why would you want to humiliate another person like that? How would you feel if it was you being physically beaten and the footage put on social media. Workplaces can also be where physical aggression and violence is used, maybe to make a co worker feel threatened and intimidated. This again can be for reasons such as wanting the victim to do the bully's work, or the bully being jealous of their victim's work promotion or relationships they may be involved in.

Physical bullying in relationships can include family members and married couples bullying each other.
Depending on the situation of the people involved, males and females can both be bullies and victims. This can be from siblings being jealous of each other, married couples or partners where one person knows the only way they will get something they want to do is to use physical force. In adult relationships this may be not allowing the other person to wear what they wish to wear or to see who they wish to see. The bully may also believe that they are entitled to sexual pleasures. Controlling money and making decisions give the bully power and if challenged, force can be used to make the victim scared and vulnerable so they allow the bully to get their own way.

Physiological Bullying

This is where the bully uses words and no hands on action to control their victim basically by playing mind games with them. They can use rude and offensive verbal language to abuse and frighten their victim and leave them intimidated along with the fear that physical violence may follow. This can happen mostly when there are no witnesses to hear or see what is going on. Sometimes there may be a witness but that person may also be too afraid to speak out or sadly a friend of the bully and does not want them to get into trouble.

By this form of bullying there are no visible signs of abuse, unlike physical bullying where bruises and body marks may be seen. This however, does by no means indicate that physiological bullying is less harmful or damaging to the sufferer. The bully carries out acts or verbal threats to frighten the victim. Therefore, leaving the victim feeling many emotions from being scared, being tearful, being nervous or even feeling angry. There may be times when nothing happens then suddenly the mind games begin again, leaving the victim wondering if or when the torture will stop.

No form of bullying is ever acceptable. But sadly this does happen.

Different reasons contribute to physiological bullying ranging from a person wanting to have more power over an individual. Some situations maybe that they know a secret that the other person never wants others to know and so the bully can blackmail them. This may not always be for money or favours but to build their ego and inflate their personal belief of power over the victim. The bully may also get pleasure by embarassing the victim in front of family members, friends or in public places or even in their own home.

When a person is experiencing the pain and humiliation of physiological bullying they can develop doubts about their own self worth and opinions and options on how to deal with the situation, which can understandably lead to low self esteem and depression. The bully can be in all life roles that we engage in. For instance, in education from fellow students, to work colleagues and within personal relationships. Sometimes, a person may not feel this is happening to them. For example, in relationships if they control what you wear, who you talk to you, where you can go and who with, yes they may have their views but are they actually ignoring your views and enforcing theirs?

If you are experiencing being physically or physiologically bullied then you need to get help and the situation sorted out as fast as you can. It may sound strange but sometimes actually talking to the bully can sort the issues out. However, if the situation does not go as planned then you have other options. You can tell your family and friends and if you cannot get their support then approach appropriate people. If it is happening in education, approach a teacher or a counsellor which is usually provided. If at work talk to your manager or other people in HR or to the owners to get this unpleasant situation resolved. In relationships you must urgently talk to whomever is bullying you, again if not stopping approach family and friends.

Finally, on physical and physiological bullying it is often found that the bully has experienced being the victim of bullying themselves. Therefore, if you are the bully you will know first hand the damage you are doing to someone else. Please stop it! Moreover, if you are the bully then you also need to work out a solution for help. A positive outlook on the awful experience of being bullied is that the victim is never to blame or is not a bad person. Even if the victim may not be physically stronger they may be emotionally stronger. Bullying is never acceptable and a solution for both the bully and the victims should urgently be found.

Pregnancy

What should be a wonderful natural experience to become pregnant and to give birth to a healthy wanted child is sadly not always going to happen. Some may find it hard to believe that a mother could suffer from depression from pregnancy.

Not every person will suffer but even if a small amount of people do they themselves still need support more than ever as becoming parents is life changing. Even if a pregnancy and childbirth go very well and the child or children is healthy in some cases depression can still arise. During pregnancy the mother can experience feelings of depression due to the change in natural hormones.

There are different stages that depression can alter the mother's wellbeing.

The antenatal stage is during pregnancy and up to the time of giving birth. During this time, the mother can sadly suffer from signs of depression, such as feeling irritable, low self esteem, tearful or being overwhelmed, this is known as antenatal depression.

Sometimes, these feelings are overlooked as just being part of being pregnant especially if it is the mother's first pregnancy. When antenatal depression is recognised the father, family and friends can give the mother the support and reassurance to reduce these unwanted feelings. There are always the wonderful doctors, midwives, maternity nurses and district nurses who can share their knowledge and experience of how to deal with these feelings. Once the baby or babies have been born this really should be such a wonderful time for celebration.

Sadly, due to different circumstances for example on how well the birth went, the babies or the mother's health can also have a dramatic impact on the mothers wellbeing. From physical changes to the mother's body to emotional feelings and reactions it really can have the mother experiencing some negative feelings rather than feeling on top of the world. Sometimes, called The Baby Blues, the feelings of being tearful, tired and problems sleeping can start after giving birth and in most cases last up to a couple of weeks.

Sadly, if feelings last longer and may include not only baby blue emotions but a lack of bonding with the newborn, loss of enjoyment in life, even with family around and a change in appetite, feeling exhausted or even anger this does not mean that you are not a wonderful, loving mother, it just means you need to be strong and talk about your feelings for support.

Strange as some people may find it fathers can also suffer from depression during all stages of the mother's pregnancy and after birth. A father may become overwhelmed with being a parent but also negative thoughts and fears can make them become depressed. Fathers, not wanting to feel silly or weak, wrongly bottle up their emotions as mainly embarrassed or not wanting to worry the mother and panic her. The Fathers can experience feelings of guilt in case the mother suffers any pain during pregnancy, worrying that the pregnancy and birth will go well, financial worries with coping with a child and the worry of how good a father they will be.

Honestly it is always best if the marriage or relationship is strong enough that you can support each other. You can, if you feel confident enough, tell your partner of your feelings. If you cannot tell them instead you could confide in family and friends or seek help from your GP. Being a parent is a wonderful feeling and responsibility that you will love and enjoy. However, depression will not let you enjoy this role like you should, therefore, talk, find support and become a healthy, happy and wonderful parent.

Termination of pregnancy by choice

This is a very sensitive and important subject. It can split and divide partners, families, politicians, even countries. Until all facts are known and understood, maybe not respected by some, I feel it is unfair for people to pass judgement without knowing why the pregnancy is to be terminated. My personal feelings are that it is up to the parents/mother to make this important decision.

The reason for this decision varies but to the pregnant person their decision to have a termination is the parents/mother and hopefully depending on the reasons they will have to consider all options and outcomes available. I am listing a few reasons and I realise this may anger some readers, however, my aim is not to anger or upset people but to help deal with circumstances that may lead to depression. If this subject or any in this chapter is the reason people are suffering from any form of depression then I hope people realise I am not judging them, I am just trying to positively help them. Not every person wishes to become a parent so their decision should be respected.

As mentioned there are many reasons why a person would consider a termination of pregnancy by choice. Health issues are a major reason for the termination of a pregnancy both for the welfare of the mother and the unborn child. One reason could be that the pregnancy was a result of an affair and the mother does not want to continue with the pregnancy as she does not want to lose her partner. Another reason could be that the pregnancy was caused by a rape. In this instance the victim may not wish to tell anyone and wants to keep the event and subsequent termination a secret. A further reason for a termination may be the age of the mother (from a very young teenager to a mature lady). Two further reasons could be financial and the mother/parents are not able to see that they can afford the child. Health is a major reason for the termination of a pregnancy both of the mother and the unborn child.

Once a pregnancy has been terminated by choice the mother and indeed father may dwell on the decision that they have made. In some cases they may feel the decision was the wrong one and this can lead to a state of guilt which can lead to depression. If you have recently made the hard decision to terminate a pregnancy this does not make you a bad person, you need and deserve love and support, please find it within your family, friends, GP or support groups mentioned in Chapter 10.

Miscarriage

For any pregnant woman, being so excited about being pregnant then to have the heartache of suffering a miscarriage is just heartbreaking and cruel. There can be certain factors why this awful event happened and hopefully it may be a one off and the couple may wish to try to conceive again and hopefully be successful.

If this unwanted experience occurs, some people find it hard to accept or can feel failures or blame themselves. Please do not do this. I know people who have cruelly suffered a miscarriage and have hearts of gold and are truly loving and amazing people. No matter what the reasons for the miscarriage it is a devastating event in a mothers/family life and can lead to guilt that the mother "did something wrong" which in turn could lead to depression.

IVF (In Vitro Fertilisation)

This is the technique that is used to help couples become parents when they are struggling to do so naturally. In this instance IVF may be their best chance of being parents. For whatever reason, becoming pregnant may not be happening; and couples should never blame themselves or each other. They should both support each other.

Sometimes, miracles do happen and when people believe that they will never become parents, pregnancy can just happen and they actually do become parents. Sadly IVF treatment does not always work and the roller coaster of emotions of going through the IVF process can be detrimental to the parents wellbeing both physically and emotionally. Experiencing failed attempts of IVF and not being pregnant may introduce episodes of depression. In such cases please find the support you need to help you through this difficult time.

Sexuality

What has generally been believed is that a man should love a woman and a woman should love a man. For centuries this has not always been followed and new generation same sex relationships are much more common, if not always understood or accepted. Maybe you have had a relationship with the opposite sex or encountered a same sex relationship and did not feel fulfilled and relaxed in either situation. Maybe you are worrying about nothing and have just not found your true love yet, whatever their sex. Sexual encounters with the opposite sex may just be covering up your true sexuality of being gay or even bi sexual. In the same way, you may have experienced same sex encounters but realise you are straight and prefer the opposite sex.

Some people are afraid to express their sexuality. This can be for a number of reasons, for example believing they will bring shame on their family, religion or culture. Not being accepted by friends and struggling with peer pressure. Afraid of being a victim of bullying or violence. Not being respected or understood by people who know them. This can leave the individual sadly, living a lie and being in denial and even wrongly feeling guilty.

If the individual is struggling with any of these feelings then they may experience a form of depression. These can include isolating themselves from others, suffering low self esteem, a lack of confidence and a feeling of emptiness even unloved.

Whatever your own situation is, you have to do what makes you happy and comfortable. Try to talk to your family who may not agree or understand at first but should hopefully accept and support your feelings. Maybe you have close friends you can be honest with and open up to. Please do not ever feel alone. There are many people who will listen to your feelings and help you. For instance, LGBT who will be very caring and will understand what you're going through. Contact details are in Chapter 10.

Body Image

Most people would love to have what is perceived to be the perfect body. However, what is a perfect body? The answer is different for all of us. For instance, some people love big muscles, others do not. Some people love body tattoos, others do not. Some people like certain hair colour, others do not. Along with body size we all may have different ideas of what the perfect body is.

The media tries to influence society to have the perfect figure but what is that? Being slender or how some people see themselves like others may be thin, skinny or anorexic or on the other hand a full figured person may be seen as large, fat or obese. In reality there is no "perfect body".

The most important thing is not the beauty on the outside but the beauty, kindness and love on the inside. Unfortunately, some people struggle with the perception of what society believes we should look like. Individuals may feel pressured in changing their body image so as to fit in. The emotional pressure of trying to have the "perfect body" can have a negative effect on a person's wellbeing. This can bring on the feelings of low self esteem, lack of confidence, change in eating habits and many other emotions. All these symptoms may lead to depression.

Addictions

There are three pastimes that can turn into very serious addictions that can take over and control your life, along with having an effect on your family and friends and your work life. These are gambling, drugs and alcohol. There can be different reasons why a person becomes addicted to anything, yet one can spiral out of control leading to becoming addicted to another or all three of these pastimes. The individual may not believe that they have a problem . It is all for enjoyment and they can stop at any time if they want to. Sadly, the individual usually says that they do not want to stop. They enjoy what they are doing and do not see a problem.

Gambling can start harmless enough, for example the odd bet or playing bingo, but this can soon spiral out of control. The individual may win small amounts and then become greedy believing that they will win a large amount of money if they place higher bets which sadly does not always happen. This can lead to money problems with the income being used to bet. This can make the individual consider borrowing or even stealing money so that they can feed their gambling habit. During this time the individual may experience mood swings, problems sleeping, change of appetite and find it hard to focus on daily tasks. These may all contribute to them suffering from depression.

An individual may use drugs and/or consume alcohol for social reasons. In some cases they may then take drugs and/or consume alcohol on a more regular basis perhaps daily or even a few times a day. This could lead to an addiction and the individual becomes dependent feeling not only does it give them enjoyment but escapism from any problems they are having in their life. When under the influence they can feel more relaxed and that life is not as bad as it really is. Sadly, this can simply be denial and this is when they have become addicted. When the effects have worn off the individual may have feelings of guilt, feel ashamed, suffer with sleeping problems and appetite changes along with mood swings which can all contribute to suffering with depression.

Anyone suffering from any of these three addictions needs to seek professional help and guidance as soon as possible.

Self Harm

Contrary to what many people believe when an individual self harms they are not always doing it for attention. They may actually be emotionally distressed or suffering with depressive episodes that have been brought on by situations for instance being bullied, struggling in education or at work, suffering with bereavement or relationship issues, to name just a few. In some cases it may be a final attempt, a cry for help, to be saved or protected.

Usually people that self harm tend to keep what they are doing and feeling to themselves. Some sufferers say they do not really know why they do it, others say when they self harm it suddenly makes them feel alive or takes their mind off the reasons that are causing them to self harm. Generally the areas which are self harmed are kept hidden away.

I have seen many people who display their self harming scars and I admit that I have been guilty of taking a second glance and always wish I could ask them how they are coping with life now.

Once an individual who was displaying her scars started talking calmly and openly to me about them. I was truly inspired how she had discovered the way to turn her life around and see her future full of confidence and positivity. She named the scars as "her body life experience markings". Telling me that when she faces a difficult situation in her life, she rubs her hands over her scars and reminds herself she can overcome anything. Bravely, and rightly so, she displayed the scars so others could see them. She told me she had hidden her scars until she saw a fellow self harmer displaying his. She was curious and asked him why he had done it. He was the first person she had spoken to about her self harming and he encouraged her to seek help, which she did. Now she still does get people, myself included, asking questions about her scars and why she self harmed.

If you have self harmed your scars are a chapter in your life book. Like the brave individual mentioned above, rub your scars when scared or down and have strength and faith like she does to know you can beat anything.

If you have self harmed and are still struggling, please find support immediately. Hopefully with your family and friends, if not your GP or any of the amazing support groups in this book.

Empty Nest Syndrome

This is when a parent has their only, last or favourite child grow up and leave home. The reasons children leave home vary, but some examples are, going to university, a career location move or a relationship being taken to the next level of moving in together. When the day arrives for the child to leave home not only will it be full of fear and excitement and responsibilities for the child but the parent will also have many mixed emotions.

The parents will, of course, be proud of what a wonderful young adult they have raised and what a wonderful life they are embarking on. But they may also have some unwanted negative feelings and emotions. In fairness the parents have spent a number of years loving, caring, supporting and doing so much for their child their leaving home will leave a huge gap in the parents lives. When a child leaves home it does not necessarily mean that they no longer love or need their parents, it just means it is time for them to fly the nest. Even though hopefully they will keep in touch and return home for visits, the parents can still struggle accepting that their child has left home. This can lead to the parent feeling abandoned, fear of their child's safety, the parent feeling tearful, lonely, experiencing mood swings and sleep issues. All of these symptoms can lead to depression if gone untreated.

PTSD (Post Traumatic Stress Disorder)

This is when a person is involved in or a witness to a disturbing horrific event that they cannot erase from their mind and therefore it has an affect on their wellbeing.

People in any of the armed forces or emergency services will come face to face with loss of life through different circumstances. How they cope and deal with the situation can affect their daily lives and wellbeing. A person does not have to work in any of the above services to be involved in a horrific event just being in the wrong place at the wrong time can mean being involved in a disturbing event.

The sufferer can struggle with many emotions including concentration problems, low self esteem, or sleeping problems due to having nightmares and flashbacks to the event. These symptoms can have a knock on effect on the person's daily life where they may not interact so well with others, becoming nervous, tearful or experience mood swings. Left untreated these conditions may lead to depression.

Don't Hold Me
Don't Support Me
Just Leave Me Alone

Sorry
I really Mean

Please Hold Me
Please Support Me
Please Stay With Me

Chapter 4
Type of Depression

There are various levels of depression. These are from mild, moderate to severe. Depending on the level of depression a person is suffering from depends how their daily life will be affected, for how long and the medication or treatment that they may require.

Some forms of depression can go unnoticed as just having a bad day or feeling a little sad or low. At some point in our lifetime this may happen to us all. Every day cannot be just fun and laughter due to modern society and our lifestyles. We are all faced with situations that can make us feel sad sometimes. This does not mean that there is any concern for thinking we have depression and life will always feel this way.

Generally, we feel much happier within a couple of days with our happy lives continuing as normal. However, what happens if these negative feelings do not improve for at least two weeks? Do we think it is not that bad and things will simply get better? Do we think we are just tired and we will feel better soon?

Sadly, many people think this way and it is totally wrong. If you experience negative emotions, thoughts and feelings for two weeks or more you should seek professional medical advice. Hopefully, it may just be a bad patch that you are going through and will resolve itself and will go as quickly as it arrived. However, such feelings each day for two weeks or more could sadly mean forms of depression can be the cause that are affecting your daily wellbeing. Therefore, please make an appointment to see your GP as soon as possible and explain your experiences.

With nearly all levels of depression the emotions are the same. It is not until the severity of the level of depression increases will there be some differences in the symptoms which are being experienced. Furthermore, the longer you leave the symptoms the worse they can get and the worse you will be feeling. You cannot correctly self diagnose what level of depression you are experiencing. Make an appointment and get the professional advice that you need to help you. The earlier you see a GP the better they can diagnose the level of depression that you may have. Some levels of depression can overlap from mild to moderate, moderate to severe depending on symptoms from person to person. If you are experiencing any of the following for two weeks or longer, please make an appointment to see your GP. Such symptoms include feeling angry, empty, frustrated, guilty, helpless, lonely, sad, tearful, tired, unloved, feeling worthless, sleeping problems, unable to concentrate, lack of interest in hobbies and withdrawn from family and friends.

Do not be frightened, embarrassed or ashamed of experiencing depression. It is experienced by many people. Remember there is not a certain type of person it affects, all human beings can suffer from depression - so you are never alone.

Those close to you may be suffering in silence and you may have no idea. If you are the sufferer please no longer stay silent, seek support and help.

SAD (Seasonal Affective Disorder)

This is a depressive condition that usually occurs in the winter months when there are less hours of daylight. Darker mornings and darker, earlier evenings can affect some people's daily moods and interest in life therefore having a negative effect on their wellbeing. Symptoms that may then occur are for example, sleeping problems, lack of energy and poor motivation. If this is how you feel over the winter months for at least two weeks please go and visit your GP for advice. This condition has similarities to mild depression so a GPs professional diagnosis is important. SAD like other forms of depression if not treated in the early stages can deteriorate into deeper depressive conditions.

Bi Polar

A well known form of depression is bi-polar. However, what is not always known is it is not only one form of depression there are two levels of bi-polar. These are called bi-polar 1 and bi-polar 2. Although they have many feelings and symptoms in common they also have extreme severity differences.

Please be reassured with support and guidance, medication, counselling and a healthy lifestyle bi polar 1 and 2, although at times very frightening for the sufferer and close family and friends, can be controlled and the sufferer can enjoy a normal life.

Bi Polar 1

Bi Polar 1 is identified if a person experiences what is known as manic episodes, which last 7 days or more. A manic episode is when the person experiences excessive amounts of high energy, they can become extremely happy, can even behave differently and participate in irrational dangerous pursuits of adrenaline excitement. Other behaviour can make them feel and act very important and superior to others. Their sleeping patterns can alter as they become restless due to their erratic behaviour during these episodes. At this point the sufferer runs a risk of being hospitalised if they put their own life at risk or that of harming others through the actions and behaviour the manic episodes may have taken them on. It is only in extreme circumstances that hospitalisation may be required. With Bi Polar 1 there are extremes of opposite feelings and behaviour. These go from the manic high energy to the total opposite of the negative extreme of depression, which leaves the sufferer feeling sad, worthless and with little or no interest in day to day routines or an interest in anything.

Bi Polar 2

Although with this condition the sufferer also experiences high and low mood swings they are slightly different to Bi Polar 1. The duration of each episode and severity will vary from person to person. Bi Polar 2 sufferers do experience more and longer lasting episodes of depressive feelings, such as feeling worthless, feeling unwanted, feeling guilty and having little energy or enthusiasm for anything.

Sometimes, these negative and persistent feelings of depression can leave a person with suicidal thoughts which may lead to them attempting to take their own life. If you are suffering from suicidal thoughts then please seek help immediately.

Schizophrenia

This is a severe form of depression that is very intense and heartbreaking to witness and sole destroying to have one's own body turn against itself. Schizophrenia affects the person's thinking, feelings and behaviour.
They can lose touch with reality and experience delusions such as believing someone is watching them, or occupying other rooms in their home and making noises. They can become paranoid believing that people do not like them or even believe people see them as evil.

Sadly, they can suffer from hallucinations believing what they can see is real when in reality it does not exist. If you or if anyone you know has any of these symptoms please immediately contact a GP. The correct treatment of medication and counselling and a healthy lifestyle may be enough to help control this medical condition.

I just want to hide in my bed
Hide from the world
Hidden I feel warm and safe
I just want time to pass me by
Until I am strong enough to stop covering up my
problems

Chapter 5
Medication

Medication is a term given for medicine that is prescribed to help a person who is suffering from any form of illness. It is given when their body cannot control and stop the illness itself naturally on its own. Once a diagnosis has been established the appropriate medication can be prescribed to help treat, ease, control, improve and hopefully cure the symptoms. Legally prescribed medication is generally prescribed by a registered general practitioner or other registered medical professionals. Depending on what the patient is suffering from and how severe the condition is depends on what medication would be prescribed. Symptoms of depression ranging from mild, moderate to severe levels will require different types of medication. The length of time that medication is required for will also vary. It is always recommended that whatever level of depression a person is suffering with needs to be diagnosed and controlled in a way that is positive and safe to the sufferer.

WARNING! WARNING! WARNING!

Please make sure that you never use another person's medication. This is very dangerous! Even if you may be suffering from the same condition, taking other people's medication can have serious side effects.

Medications that help and heal one person may react differently to others especially if they are already taking other medication. The other person may also have been prescribed a higher dosage than may have been prescribed to you. This is why you must only take medication legally prescribed to you and you alone. Even with this said what a GP can prescribe can still give you side effects, which will all be mentioned on the medication, if you do experience any of the side effects contact whomever prescribed the medication as they may suggest you stop taking the medication immediately and have a further consultation for a different medication to help you. If you feel that you are benefiting from the prescribed medication, complete the course and before you do finish the course you may wish to make a follow up appointment to discuss your medication and wellbeing going forward.

All different stages of depression ranging from mild to moderate to severe can be helped by the taking of prescribed medication.

Hopefully if you are the sufferer you may have a good idea of the reason or reasons that are changing your positive wellbeing feelings to that of negative feelings and emotions causing the depressive symptoms.

Sometimes, we do not either want to admit them or do not realise there may be many until we talk about our feelings and look at our life situation. When you speak to a medical professional it is not law that you have to take their advice or suggested medication but I would suggest that it would be wise to, this is due to their knowledge and expertise. They only want to help you improve your wellbeing. For example, for mild cases of depression you may be advised that before taking any medication a few lifestyle changes could be made to naturally improve your health and help control your depressive feelings.

Normally such changes would include a healthier diet which plays a very important role in your body's physical and emotional wellbeing. Also regular daily exercise is wonderful to stimulate natural feel good hormones to promote a positive attitude to life. Along with diet and exercise sleep is very important and this is discussed more in Chapter 8.

Medications mostly given to people suffering with depression are known as antidepressants. Medication is to help control your depressive episodes, sadly, it cannot make your problems simply go away and disappear forever.

The timescale and level of medication given will depend on the individual and their symptoms. The medication will not work instantly but over the following weeks and months an improvement should be felt. You may find it of benefit to keep a daily journal to record any side effects from the medication taken, do you feel an improvement in your wellbeing, any physical or emotional feelings you have experienced for better or worse, sleeping patterns, appetite, concentration as just some examples. By recording these details it will be a good guide on how the medication may or may not be helping you. By recording your feelings this will assist your GP in observing your progress and will help the GP know if the medication is suitable for your needs.

An alternative to prescribed medication for mild depression is the option of herbal medication. The first form of medication was all natural as this was man's only option and so was used to try to heal and cure all diseases, illnesses and infections.

Now the modern conventional drugs are synthetically made and not all natural, people do sometimes prefer natural over conventional medication. With natural medication they use the plants roots, leaves and petals. Certain plants have been traditionally used, in parts of the world, for centuries to help with the wellbeing of the body. A GP may be able to give advice on natural medicine. The GP may point out that it is just as important to take the correct amount of natural medication as it is the conventional medication. Also it is not always recommended to take the two forms together in case they give you a bodily reaction. The GP may advise that the conventional medication is made in laboratories to legal regulations that are monitored and recorded to the same quality in every batch. Natural medicines may not always guarantee this high level quality control as nature naturally varies. Natural medicines do not have such high regulation requirements to meet as conventional medicines do.

If you would like to try natural medicine apart from a GP a pharmacist or herbal practitioner would be the best people to speak to on how natural medication may help your depression.

By visiting your GP increases the success rate for your depression to be controlled. Whatever option you chose you have made a brave start seeking medical advice and help. The process may seem slow at times but the positive happy times which lay ahead will be worth it.

Chapter 6
Counselling & Therapy

Once you have been strong enough and brave enough to accept you are experiencing depressive feelings hopefully you will go to your GP. Whilst with your GP you will be able to explain your feelings and thoughts on how depression is affecting your wellbeing.   Hopefully the appointment will find a positive solution that should improve your wellbeing. Your GP may refer you to counselling.   A recent study indicates that a person suffering from depressive feelings who was taking prescribed medication along with seeing a counsellor had a positive improvement on their wellbeing. If your GP does recommend you see a counsellor they may refer you via the NHS who offer a talking therapy service. Your GP may also inform you that there are private counsellors that you can see for a fee. Another option is that some areas have support groups that sometimes offer free counselling sessions for young adults.

If for any reason your GP does not feel you need to receive counselling you can, of course, still obtain counselling should you feel that this would be beneficial to you. You can refer yourself to the NHS, contact a private counsellor or even search for a local support group.

Who is a counsellor?

A counsellor is a person in one of many careers that helps people with their struggles with feelings, behaviour and emotions related to areas of depression, stress and anxiety.

BACP (British Association for Counsellor and Psychotherapy)

This is the main recognised body for practising counsellors and therapists. They make sure ethical standards to clients are maintained. The BACP also holds details of training, qualifications and can provide the counsellors or therapists with more qualifications and supervision that BACP organise. However, it is not a legal requirement to be registered with BACP; it is optional. The benefits are that the counsellor can advertise that they are registered and that their ethical standards and qualifications are recorded. In the UK without this recognition a person can still operate as a counsellor. This does not mean that they do not have high ethical standards or qualifications or experience by not becoming a member. If you find a counsellor who does not belong to BACP you may ask them why and also what qualifications and experience that they have.

Empathy

This means that the counsellor understands and respects your points of view, feelings and emotions and how they make you feel and behave. This is one of the most important reasons for choosing a person to help you. Regardless of their qualifications the most important thing is the connection between yourself and your chosen counsellor. As you become more confident in yourself along with developing trust and confidence in your counsellor a more positive outlook for your wellbeing can be developed. After your first sessions, maybe even a few, you may feel there is no empathy and decide to seek an alternative counsellor. Which is totally understandable and your decision to do.

Sessions

When you have contacted your chosen counsellor depending on how you wish to take your sessions, on line, telephone, outdoors walk and talk or face to face in a private setting. It is normal that the introductory session is free of charge.

During the initial session you can ask any questions about their qualifications and their experience of the issues you are suffering with. You may be extremely nervous and wrongfully feel embarrassed but you must feel proud of your progress to reach out for support. Different counsellors have different areas of expertise. For example, the areas of expertise range from alcohol or drug addiction, family and personal relationship problems, education and work problems, bereavement and grief, low self esteem, general depressive feelings, physical and sexual abuse to loneliness. During the introductory session the counsellor will ask you to tell them your problems and feelings. The more honest and open you are with the counsellor the easier finding the positive outcome will be. These may be about issues you have not told another person, or could be current issues you cannot cope with on your own that are harming your day to day wellbeing.

Generally a session will last for around 50 minutes to 1 hour which most people attend once a week. On average 8-16 weeks is the time taken for the client to feel confident of controlling their wellbeing in a positive day to day environment without no longer needing sessions.

Cases can vary from person to person so discussion between a counsellor and client is the best way to decide the client's best outcome for the amount of sessions required.

During sessions your current wellbeing will be discussed and compared to daily feelings since the last session. These can be negative or positive, you just have to be honest as it helps you find positive solutions faster by being honest. Your actions and behaviour will also be discussed. Your counsellor will help you set realistic achievable goals. During sessions you may also discuss your opinions on how the current session is going and how the previous session went.

A counsellor may ask you to do some homework, by keeping a daily journal covering your negative and positive emotions, feelings, behaviour and activities you may have experienced throughout any particular day. You can discuss this during your next session whatever the findings.

Evidence shows more people find stronger positive results by completing the homework whilst taking these sessions. By doing this generally the client can develop coping skills better by looking at what they have written seeing the evidence and feelings in front of them. This does help them focus on what has happened and stimulates them to realise they can change negative feelings to positive solutions. During further sessions you may discover you have other issues, which you thought would not need to have been brought up or did not realise were harming your wellbeing. As each session is held, the main focus on your problems that were causing you depressive feelings will be discussed.

Through the experience, support and guidance of the counsellor and your determination to beat depression a positive outcome can be achieved.

The counsellor and client can set realistic goals which can be achieved to improve the client's wellbeing. For example, this can be done by the client becoming a volunteer, helping in the local community or pursuing a new interest. These can all help with social interaction which is very important to an individuals wellbeing. Hopefully these goals can be achieved and new target goals discussed and arranged.

During continuing sessions your confidence and wellbeing should improve and give feelings of a positive outlook for the future. As usual in these sessions you can have an input to discuss your feelings and developments that occur under the guidance of the counsellor. Along with your counsellor you will eventually discuss your progress and when you both feel happy and confident to arrange when your last session should be. This should happen when all areas that have affected your wellbeing have been discussed and resolved.

CBT (Cognitive Behavioural Therapy)

Many counsellors use CBT, a form of talking therapy, to help their client's control and overcome the experiences of depression. CBT basically tries to turn negative thoughts into positive thoughts. It aims to teach the client different ways of looking at problems, behavioural actions and emotions and change their handling of these situations. It helps teach and develop different coping skills for a positive outlook.

Art Therapy

If an individual has difficulty in discussing emotions and problems verbally there are a number of alternative methods of support. One such option is Art Therapy. A qualified therapist in Art Therapy can be a wonderful solution in helping people express their feelings and emotions through forms of art work. Some people find it almost impossible to talk about the reasons and experiences that are causing them to feel depressed. Art Therapy helps the individual express their feelings and emotions creatively through art. The therapist will offer a range of materials to be used including drawing, painting and clay work which tend to be the most popular. By using materials it helps the individual to try and express the causes of their problems in the work that they create. The art therapist may ask questions to try and help the individual discuss their work and what it relates to. By taking art therapy it encourages the person to look at what they see as the causes of their depression.

Art Therapy will hopefully leave the individual feeling relaxed and boosting their confidence and self esteem as they are finally finding a solution that can help them. Generally Art Therapy sessions last 30-60 minutes are either weekly or fortnightly for 8-12 weeks depending on the individual's circumstances and progress. It is helpful if the individual is finally able to talk about what they have created and why. The individual can hopefully resolve whatever negative feelings they have and identify the causes of their depressive problems. Their personal creation may give them coping skills allowing them to calmly talk about the causes. The work that they have created has come from deep inside to heal them and see a positive future.

On completion of the Art Therapy sessions it may give the individual confidence to continue receiving counselling (or see their GP) on a face to face basis if they feel that this is required.

Chapter 7
Alternative Therapy

So you may have or may not have tried talking to family, friends, visiting a GP or support group or counsellor to help you with your feelings of depression.

Hopefully, you will have found guidance and benefit by using one of these options. However, if you did not try them or even if you did and felt you did not get on as well as you would have hoped, all is far from lost. For your wellbeing and future happiness you should find positive results by trying alternative therapies. You have admitted that you have a problem with depression and may not have felt relaxed or comfortable with other ways of allowing yourself to be helped. Maybe a more relaxed approach to your feeling of depression and your state of mind should be helped by the following alternative therapies.

My personal favourite, which helped me overcome depression, I call self awareness and enjoyment therapy. Denial is not healthy and only makes the suffering worse for the individual. Once you have opened up about your feelings you may feel a weight lifted off your shoulders but this does not mean that all problems are solved instantly. It would be wonderful if this was the case. However, by learning to accept and control feelings gives us the greatest chance to beat depression and to create a relaxing lifestyle.

For my self awareness and enjoyment therapy first you need to be honest with yourself and not critical or judgemental, like you may feel or others may have been towards you. Just look at yourself in the mirror, do not think in a negative way about looks and features, just smile. Praise yourself about your lovely eye colour, wonderful hair style, maybe your button nose and nice facial pimples or beauty spots. Above all smile and look how happy you can appear.

The reason I am keen to encourage you to show off your lovely smile is that you will discover that behind the smile does not always mean it is not genuine. You will, in time, smile inside and out. A smile is very important to help you feel better about life and yourself. So let's start with your smile. This is one of the feel good experiments that you can do. We all know how seeing someone happy makes people feel good. Laughter is a wonderful sound and a feeling that you can never get enough of. So when you next go out and people are coming towards you just simply give them a lovely smile.

When you come into contact with people, be that your friends and family, the person helping you in the supermarket, the barista in your favourite coffee shop greet them with a Good Morning, Good Afternoon or a simple hello and a smile. This will make you feel good about yourself and others. You may not always get a positive response but in general you will receive a lot of smiles and replies. By these actions not only have you made yourself feel good by being friendly and polite but you will also have made the recipient happy with your greeting.

Sometimes, little acts may seem pointless but meeting people and having interaction with them is a very good way to lift a person's morale when suffering from depression. Your smile is a great natural action that you will find makes you and others happy.

Being outside, admiring the countryside and being with nature and in open spaces can help free our minds from our day to day lives. Go to a nice quiet place where you can relax and unwind. Close your eyes, take a deep breath and inhale and exhale a few times before opening your eyes and enjoying the beautiful surrounding area, look up at the clouds and watch them gently moving. Now focus and imagine what shapes they can form, let your imagination run wild. Maybe you can visualise a dog, a fish, a car or even a tree basically anything it is your imagination there is no right or wrong. This is for you to appreciate what beauty is around you.
How marvellous nature is and how good it can make you feel. Close your eyes once again and breathe in and out slowly then open your eyes. I am sure wherever you are viewing the sky you will see how wonderful the sky and scenery really are. These views are around us but do we ever really take the time to appreciate them? This is your time. We can all take a short break from our daily routine to improve our wellbeing. The lovely fresh air helps you to feel calm, breathing deep and slowly to slow your heartbeat, you can and should do this every day and it is all free and natural and will make you feel good.

The most amazing and natural sights to see, in my opinion, is a sunrise or a sunset. Just viewing them, wherever you may be, has always made me feel calm and relaxed and realise that life is a special gift to appreciate. It made me understand that my problems could not be solved all at once but there was always another day to look forward to.

Another favourite of my enjoyment and awareness therapies is simply observing animals in nature. Depending on where you live will depend on what animals you have to observe. I am lucky enough to live in the countryside so when I observe nature I get to see deer, birds, and other countryside animals. Maybe you can see birds and tempt them with some food. Hopefully they will feel safe and may approach you to eat what you have tempted them with. By feeding them please do not think that they are just eating, relax and observe them, watch how they move their bodies, and check to see if it is safe enough to come close to the food without threat or danger. Look at their characteristics, are they brave, strong or just a bit cheeky. Look how they all move differently due to their sizes and their feet. The different colours at different angles of their feathers. Their different eyes. Just take a few minutes to relax and really observe any animals that you can see as you will find by concentrating on these animals and how unique their behaviour patterns are will make you relax and unwind and appreciate nature. It is always very rewarding and I always found it a nice place to escape to which made me feel calm, safe and at peace with myself.

Just be aware that some animals will eat almost anything when hungry; however, it is much healthier for animals to eat foods as close to their natural diets as possible. Certain nuts and seeds would be much healthier to feed to birds and squirrels.

These animals will not judge you, they will just be grateful for your kindness. You could make this a regular thing to do, good for you and good for nature.

If you attend the same locations regularly, you will notice and appreciate the change in scenery and the plants throughout the seasons. All seasons are important: Winter, Spring, Summer and Autumn. The growing of leaves, bulbs flowering and birds nesting and feeding. All seasons are beautiful in their own way. My favourite season is autumn as I love the amazing colours as the leaves change ready to drop for winter. What is your favourite season and why?

Remember being outside and connecting with others and nature is essential for our wellbeing. You will truly discover how being outside really helps you, a walk and fresh air are so good for your mind and body.

If you enjoy photography or painting you may wish to consider visiting the same location throughout the year and recording how the scenery changes.

Smile - it is natural

Nature makes you smile

Before I mention other alternative therapies that are very popular and beneficial I would like to really let you know the many wonderful benefits of gardening. This is a healthy, rewarding activity which is very therapeutic. There are so many reasons why you may enjoy gardening. Even though you may think that you do not have a garden suitable to grow things in, all is not lost. If there is no outside space you may have indoor space somewhere where you can get the benefit of plants, herbs and flowers. Any room, windowsill, balcony or door entrance may be suitable. Fresh flowers will not only look lovely in your home, they have the added benefit of smelling sweet and have positive factors of calming and relaxing people. Low maintenance plants for example cacti and succulents are very easy to keep and add a natural feature to any room. Growing herbs in your kitchen not only provides fresh and healthy cooking ingredients, it brings colour and fragrance to your home. Like myself, all people who love gardening will agree, gardening truly is wonderful for your mind, body and soul.

Just being outside in the fresh air is beneficial for you. A true gardener will tell you, no matter what the weather, there is always something to do. This can range from planting, pruning, weeding and digging or even just pottering about and tidying up. The real beauty is that at the end of the day all your time spent working in the garden will reap rewards be it in the produce you have grown or the enjoyment of nurturing your plants and watching them grow. Hopefully, you will enjoy your work in the garden, sometimes physical work but this is a good form of exercise and helps you to keep fit.

Research has proven that digging and planting not only makes you focus on what you are doing but it can take away negative thoughts that can contribute towards depression and instead creates positive thoughts and feelings. This is because inside the soil are microbes which when breathed in can stimulate the bodies natural anti depression chemical Serotonin. Gardening is, therefore, very important for your mind, body and soul. Finally, you can give something back to nature by scattering wildflower seeds in places you pass often and watch them grow for your pleasure, the pleasure of others and also for the wildlife to enjoy.

The alternative therapies mentioned really have helped me whilst I was suffering from depression and helped me regain the happy healthy lifestyle I was missing. I truly hope that you find the same pleasure and rewarding outcome as I did.

Yoga

This is a very popular spiritual discipline. You may wish to practise yoga on your own or by attending a class, the choice is entirely yours. By joining a class you will have an instructor giving you in depth guidance and support along with meeting other people for social interaction.

Yoga is very good for your health and helps with personal relaxation. It uses meditation which helps you to clear your mind, relax and uses special calming breathing techniques which will help you focus and improve your concentration ability.

Being calm, focused and being able to concentrate better will help you manage awkward situations more easily. The art of yoga not only focuses on meditation and breathing but includes standing and sitting poses. Regular yoga exercises will strengthen your core and body muscles allowing you to become more flexible and also stronger. You will discover that you can control your body by using conscious control of your mind.

Other benefits of yoga include improving your blood circulation, reducing blood pressure which also helps with lowering the feelings of depression. Yoga is not only good for your joint movements it builds up an appetite for you so hopefully a healthy diet may be followed. It is also good to help you improve your sleep pattern. So before you go to bed, 10-15 minutes of yoga with a controlled gentle breathing technique can help you end your day calmer and hopefully improve the quality of your sleep.

The same method at the start of the day: a gentle movement of exercise and controlled breathing can help you begin your day in a calm and focused way.

Meditation

Meditation is a great way to help a person relax and unwind. The art of meditation is to help the individual focus their mind on a certain positive activity, thought or feeling. By being relaxed and blocking out any negative or unwanted thoughts and feelings you can make yourself simply focus on your positive selection. You let your body become a free spirit, this way it will help you enjoy your meditation experience a lot more.

The aim is to focus on your selected image and try to keep all concentration just on that image to receive the best benefits possible from your meditation. By doing this you will become much more aware and focused on life around you. Practising meditation regularly will help you to find a deeper inner peace. This itself will help you control and focus on situations better than you usually would. You will find by doing meditation regularly your concentration will increase and you will become calmer. Like yoga it can be studied on your own but taking classes and receiving professional guidance can be a more beneficial alternative.

Massage

Another alternative therapy that is a wonderful rewarding treatment is massage. I use the word rewarding as you like myself when you have worked so hard and have really tried to feel comfortable and relaxed and feel impressed on how you control your depressive feelings a reward is greatly required. A massage is a manual therapy where the therapist manipulates the body's muscles and helps soreness, tired muscles and tension. It also helps improve blood flow and circulation, boosts energy and alertness along with lowering the heart beat and blood pressure levels in the short term.

When you have found a qualified masseuse that you feel relaxed with, they are certainly worth going to whenever you feel the need for pampering yourself. After you have experienced this wonderful relaxing therapy you should feel like you are walking on air. Your stress should be reduced after you have allowed your body to unwind and be treated. If possible you could go regularly as we all deserve to feel good and relaxed.

Hugs

A hug is one of the best natural feelings we can give and receive and something that we are all capable of giving and the recipient will also be grateful for the hug.

Chapter 8
Diet, Exercise & Sleep

This chapter aims to show that a healthy diet, regular exercise and a good sleep pattern will all help you to control your depression and improve your wellbeing.

Diet

Diet means what we put into our bodies by consuming different foods and liquids. Are there any rights and wrongs? Surely each individual has the right to choose what they have to eat and drink. Technically to a degree we do have the option to choose what we consume. However, due to some religious and/or personal beliefs and choices some people may choose to follow a restricted diet. Others may have special medical needs that restrict them from consuming certain foods.

If you enjoy it, surely that is good? That does sound correct, however the answer can also be no. The reason being that we are told and know that a healthy balanced diet is much better for our bodies and therefore better for our minds than the intake of processed junk food, carbonated drinks and alcohol.

Water is needed by every person and is important to whichever diet you may follow, we cannot live without it. It carries out many functions to help keep our body healthy. These range from taking nutrients and oxygen to all our body cells, it flushes out bodily fluids through urine and helps with bowel movements. It helps with digestion and the lubrication of our joints. When we have enough water in our bodies we are hydrated. This is very important as being hydrated helps our brain and body function better. Being dehydrated can give you headaches, make you feel tired, restrict bowel movements, affect concentration and alertness. A wonderful water fact is that water is 60% of your body weight.

There are a number of diets which are available but here are just a few. A meat, fish, fruit and vegetable diet known as omnivore diet, a vegetarian diet and a vegan diet.

One healthy combination of fruit and vegetables that should be followed on all diets is 5 a day. It is recommended to combine fruit and vegetables of five different types to help keep our bodies in good health by the intake of vitamins and minerals. How much counts as a 1 of the 5 a day? The recommended weight should be 80 gms of each different choice. Eating more than 80 gms of one particular fruit or vegetables still only counts towards 1 of the 5 a day. Therefore, you need five selections of at least 80 gms for a total of 400 gms roughly 14 ozs in total for your daily requirements of 5 a day. Please be aware that potatoes are not included within the 5 a day plan.

For the meat and fish diet followers there are four main food groups where their foods are taken from:-

Fruit and vegetables
This group is low in fat and provides the body with important vitamins and minerals. The intake of these helps with the body's digestive system along with keeping our immune system strong and healthy. Although dried fruit and fruit juices are good for you it is best to keep to a restricted consumption as they are high in sugars which are not good for the body in regular high intakes.

Carbohydrates
These are a good form of energy for the body. They are found in whole grain pasta, whole grain breakfast cereals, whole grain oats and bread, pitta bread and chapati. Another carbohydrate that is cooked in many different forms and is good for energy is the potato.

Dairy
This group includes products such as milk, yogurt and cheese all of which are very important in supplying our bodies with protein and calcium which are needed to develop and maintain strong teeth and bones.

Protein

This is found in all meats and poultry and also in oil rich fish such as salmon, mackerel and sardines. Sea food, also high in protein, includes oysters, mussels and crab. Eggs and greek yogurt are also recommended for protein intake. By eating any of these our body uses the protein to develop and strengthen our muscles and protein also helps with body growth along with body repair.

By enjoying these food groups and eating recommended portion sizes we can give our body's the best chance of staying strong and healthy.

Vegetarian Diet

This is where a person chooses not to eat meat or fish but they do choose to consume eggs and dairy products, like milk, yogurt and cheese. As a vegetarian does not eat meat and fish they will need to get their protein through other sources by eating eggs, tofu, pulses and lentils.

Vegan Diet

This is very similar to a vegetarian diet but the main difference is that vegans do not only not eat meat or fish they do not eat any animal by-products such as eggs and milk. Vegans can still have a very healthy diet they just need to find alternative non animal proteins and vitamins B12. Protein for vegan requirements are very similar to vegetarians as they include tofu, pulses, lentils. As for B12 alternative choices that meet a vegan's intake requirements are nutritional yeast and spread; these include vegemite and also shiitake mushrooms.

Vitamins and Minerals

As our body's do not naturally produce vitamins and minerals we have to consume certain foods that contain them. The following vitamins and minerals are all extremely important to our body's. They carry out very important roles to help our bodies function correctly and to remain healthy. These roles include fighting infections, maintaining strong bones and teeth, helping with blood clotting and keeping our nervous and immune system healthy.

Vitamin A

Is very important for our vision, immune system, healthy skin and helps keep our teeth and bones healthy. The best natural sources of vitamin A are found in liver, salmon, mackerel, sweet potato, broccoli, spinach and raw carrots.

B Vitamins

These are not stored by the body so they are needed to be consumed daily.

B1 Thiamine

This is a very important vitamin that uses the proteins, fats and carbohydrates that we consume and turns them into energy. It is also important for the heart, muscles and nerve functions. This vitamin is naturally found in pork, chicken, salmon, mussels, eggs, cheese, brown rice and lentils.

B2 Riboflavin

This vitamin also converts food intake into energy and is important for the body's growth along with helping to produce and protect our red blood cells. This vitamin is found naturally in liver, chicken, salmon, milk, yogurt, cheese, eggs, avocado and leafy green vegetables.

B3 Niacin

This vitamin also converts the food we consume into energy along with this it helps our digestive system function correctly and is important to keep our skin healthy. This is found in foods such as turkey, chicken, tuna, salmon, banana, whole grain and sunflower seeds.

B5 Pantothenic Acid

This vitamin breaks down carbohydrates and fats to be converted into energy for the body. It also plays an important role to produce red blood cells. The foods which contain this vitamin are beef, chicken, salmon, banana, chickpeas, soya beans and almonds.

B6 Pyridoxine

This vitamin plays an important role to keep our immune and nervous system functioning fully along with our brain development and is found in turkey, chicken, pork, tuna, potatoes and milk.

B7 Biotin

This vitamin plays a role in the function of our liver and kidneys and also plays an important role in keeping our skin, teeth and nails strong and healthy. B7 is found in liver, beef, salmon, eggs, peanuts and cauliflower.

B9 Folate
This vitamin is very important in the production of red blood cells and very important during pregnancy for the health of the baby. It can be found in liver, eggs, citrus fruits, spinach, leafy green vegetables and soya beans.

B12 Cyanocobalamin
This vitamin is not only very important in the collaboration with B9 for our DNA it is also essential in keeping the body's blood and nerve cells functioning and healthy. It can be found in lamb, chicken, salmon, trout, sardines, milk, yogurt and cheese.

Vitamin C
The importance of vitamin c is that it helps produce collagen which combined they help maintain the skin and bones also including connecting cartilage, tendons and ligaments. Vitamin C is found in virtually all citrus fruits such as oranges, grapefruit and lemons and also in tomatoes and cabbage.

Vitamin D
The main function of vitamin D is to maintain strong teeth and promote bone growth and strength. It also helps keep our immune system strong and healthy. Vitamin D can be created by being out in direct sunlight. The foods that contain vitamin D include oily fish, salmon, sardines, tuna, eggs, cheese, cows milk and soya milk.

Vitamin E

The role of vitamin E is that it keeps our immune system strong and healthy. It also contributes to forming red blood cells and helping the blood flow easily. Vitamin E is found in eggs, broccoli, asparagus, avocado, kiwi fruit, nuts and sunflower oil.

Vitamin K

This vitamin is very important for blood clotting when our blood vessels are damaged. Vitamin K can be found in leafy green vegetables, eggs, lettuce and prunes.

Minerals

The five most important minerals for our body's are iron, calcium, magnesium, zinc and potassium.

Iron

This is very important for the development and growth of our body's. Iron makes a protein known as haemoglobin in red blood cells which from the lungs transport oxygen all around our body. Iron is found in liver, beef, shellfish, oysters, dried fruit, broccoli and tomatoes.

Calcium

This is very important for the strength of the body's bones and teeth. Calcium also plays a vital role in the tensing and relaxing of our muscles as well as controlling a healthy normal heartbeat. Calcium also helps carry signals around our body from the brain. It is found in sardines, salmon, milk, cheese, yogurt, soya beans and kale.

Magnesium

The role of magnesium is to keep our bones strong and healthy. It also keeps our immune system healthy and helps with maintaining our muscle and nervous system functions. Magnesium also influences a healthy blood pressure. It is found naturally in salmon, bananas, wholegrain, brown rice and nuts.

Zinc

The main role of zinc is to keep our immune system strong and healthy. Along with this zinc also contributes to healing our damaged body tissues. Zinc is found in the following beef, chicken, oysters, shellfish, eggs, mushrooms and lentils.

Potassium

This mineral helps to maintain a healthy blood pressure level, balancing our body's PH levels of acidity and alkalinity and helping with digestion along with controlling our muscle contractions. Foods that contain potassium are bananas, salmon, yogurt, watermelon, raisins, potatoes and spinach.

Along with vitamins and minerals there is also a very important fatty acid known as omega 3 which is not produced in the body. Omega 3 plays a very important role in keeping our body healthy, especially keeping the brain functioning correctly. It is also equally important in keeping the heart functioning healthy and correctly. Omega 3 is found in oily fish and other foods such as oysters, trout, eggs, soya beans and walnuts.

Supplements
If required, a supplement tablet can be taken that will increase the intake of a certain protein, vitamin or mineral should these be lacking in a person's diet.

Exercise

It is very often correct that a healthy body leads to a healthy mind. Although we are all individuals we are all very similar. To keep our bodies healthy and functioning to their best of their abilities, exercise, like a healthy balanced diet and a regular good sleep pattern, contribute to a positive impact on our health. By different forms of exercise we can improve our fitness levels which when we are fit and healthy can help our bodies and minds become strong and positive.

Daily exercise, in some form, is recommended for everyone regardless of their current level of fitness. Daily exercise is not only good for the body but it can be good for the mind and help in reducing symptoms of depression.

The minimum recommended daily amount of time for exercise is 30 minutes.

I do realise that having depression does not make you feel like going out and doing any type of exercise when you are not feeling your usual self. Sadly, the longer you put off daily exercise the harder it will be to start.

Commitments do play a major part in when we can exercise and you will also need certain facilities for certain types of exercise. Remember you can vary the exercise that you do, it does not have to be the same each day. Just simply choose a form of exercise that you enjoy.

Once you begin to enjoy your daily exercise routine, you may wish to adjust your lifestyle to increase the amount of exercise that you do. At some point you may wish to join a club which will not only help your physical and fitness levels it will also improve your social circle. Social interaction is a great way to manage depression as it gives you a reason to go and see others.

The most popular of all exercises is probably walking. The reasons are that walking is free and a natural movement and you can walk anywhere. Another reason why walking is so good for you is not only does it allow you to go at your own pace, it makes the heart beat increase, improves the heart strength and increases blood circulation around the body.

Jogging is also a popular type of exercise. Jogging is a good way to give your body a cardiovascular workout so it gets the heart pumping the blood around the body and helps the heart become stronger. I found when I was suffering from depression by going jogging I could think of my problems and it seemed to help me think of the solutions to solve them. Sometimes I just felt like jogging and not stopping. It wasn't that I was running away from my problems, I just found it easier to focus calmly on my feelings.

Another wonderful form of exercise is swimming. This is also a great way to improve your fitness levels. Just walking in the water is very good exercise even if you do not swim.

Please remember to always stay hydrated.

All types of exercise release the natural body hormones such as endorphins and serotonin both of which contribute to your wellbeing and therefore will help reduce the symptoms of depression.

Sleep

A very important factor to help maintain a healthy wellbeing is sleep. This sadly is what many people, for various reasons, do not get enough of. We all need a peaceful, undisturbed, comfortable night's sleep. A good sleep is crucial to our wellbeing because it can lower the risks of health problems, helps with our memory, concentration and improves our mood as well as giving us a feeling of energy for the day ahead.

There are two opposite sleep conditions that people with depression can experience. Firstly, and known as insomnia is a sleep problem of not getting enough sleep or having disturbed sleeping patterns so the individual will feel restless and tired. The second condition is hypersomnia which is where the individual sleeps for excessive periods of time for example 10 hours or longer on a regular basis. Even after this long duration of sleep the individual can still feel lethargic and have a low mood feeling. With either of these conditions it is wise to seek the advice of a GP.

If you are struggling to sleep, maybe set aside 15 minutes 3 to 4 hours prior to going to bed to sort out and deal with any problems or issues that you are experiencing. During this time you may be able to find a positive solution to solve them hence giving you a free mind to unwind prior to sleep. Trying not to eat or drink too much prior to going to bed may help reduce the amount of times you wake up either with indigestion or needing the toilet. Try to turn off and ignore any mobile phones, or laptops etc by at least one hour prior to going to bed. This should help your brain switch off and relax. Your bedroom should feel like a nice relaxing, calm and safe place you love to be in to relax. Gentle soothing music is a great way to help you drift off to sleep. Many people find reading a book prior to bedtime helps improve their sleep as they focus on the words of the book rather than on the stresses of the day. Maybe prior to getting into bed practise some nice calming deep breathing exercises to clear and relax the mind.

Sweetdreams!

Chapter 9
Progress

By reading this book I hope you will see through different options we can accept, control and often beat depression. Trying to overcome any form of depression on your own can be very difficult. If you have not yet been able to talk to someone about your depressive feelings and experiences please be brave enough as talking is a great starting point to controlling your depressive feelings.

It is not a weak person
That asks for help
It is a strong and brave person
That asks for help

Once you have started talking about how you are really feeling, life slowly but surely can improve. Once you have accepted that you have depression here are some suggestions that may help you continue on a positive road to control and hopefully beat depression now and in the future.

Keeping a daily journal

By keeping a journal over a period of time, I believe you will see a positive improvement in your wellbeing. If you have had any form of counselling your counsellor may have encouraged you to keep a daily journal. It is very wise and rewarding to keep a journal. The wonderful thing about the journal is that it is 100% about you, your feelings, behaviour, experiences and how you have managed throughout the day.

How you complete your journal is up to you. However, you should record all negative and positive feelings in whatever manner you wish to be that with words, a drawing, a poem or a positive statement. For example, if someone tells you a funny joke that makes you laugh, maybe record it for future reference.

After a period of time your journal will be able to show you what days you are positive and what days you are not and the reasons that have contributed to your negative and positive feelings.

After you have kept a daily journal for a few weeks, hopefully you will feel that your wellbeing has improved.

Setting goals

Each day try to set yourself a realistic and achievable goal for example, setting aside 30 minutes within the day for yourself. Be that a walk in the park or a soak in the bath by giving yourself some personal time this will help you relax and unwind.

You may wish to set a goal to ensure that you get to school or work on time. By doing this you will start your day with less stress of being late.

Positive opposite game

If you have seen a counsellor they may have used CBT (Cognitive Behaviour Therapy) to encourage you to change negative thoughts into positive thoughts.

This is a game that you can play anywhere and at any time. Just write down some words and place them under a negative column next to the word, think of an opposite word so it becomes a positive statement. For example:-

Negative Word	Positive Word
Anger	*Calm*
Rude	*Polite*
Shy	*Confident*
Tired	*Energetic*

The list is entirely for your ideas to help you try and find positive solutions in different situations.

As *anger* is negative and not good for your wellbeing, *calm* is the positive choice. To be calm is better for your wellbeing and you can focus and handle situations better. When you are calm others prefer to interact with you as you are seen as a nicer person.

By playing this "game" this will help you understand that negative feelings are not good for your wellbeing and the alternative positive answer can be the outcome that you aim for to achieve a happier and healthier lifestyle.

Rewards

For your persistent interest in completing your daily journal and setting yourself regular goals along with the positive achievements that these have helped you accomplish, you deserve to spoil yourself. A reward can be anything that you choose for example, a meal out with family or friends, a trip to the cinema, enjoying a massage or treating yourself to something nice.

Chapter 10
Support Groups

As mentioned throughout the book here is a list of some excellent support groups who are always available to help you. Please contact any of the appropriate groups related to your wellbeing, they will offer you comfort, respect and support and will not judge you.

To the amazing staff of these groups a million thanks for doing such a wonderful job, please keep the good work up and take care of yourselves.

Samaritans
Contact number 116123
Available 24 hours a day, 365 days year
Please call them immediately if you have any suicidal thoughts.
The Samaritans are there to help in a non judgemental way when you need to speak to someone. You can discuss depression, relationship problems, drug and alcohol abuse, loneliness, financial worries and any other issues you need to talk about.

MIND
Contact number 0300 123 3393
Available Monday to Friday 9am - 6pm (excluding Bank Holidays)
For help with your mental health questions and advising on support on all mental health conditions, including supporting the person concerned and their families with alcohol and drug problems.

Young Mind
Contact number 0808 802 5544
Available Monday to Friday 9.30am to 4pm
Young Mind offers support not only for the person suffering from a mental health problem but also advice and support for concerned family and friends.

CALM (Campaign Against Living Miserably)
Contact number 0800 585858
Available 5pm - midnight 365 days a year
This charity is focused on helping males aged between 15-35 years old to avoid taking their lives by suicide.

NSPCC Childline
Contact number 0800 1111 24
Available 24 hours a day 365 days a year
For children and young people who need to talk to someone about bullying, mental or physical abuse, sexual abuse or any other problem they may be experiencing.

SHOUT
Text only to 85258
Available 24 hours a day
Text support line for individuals in a crisis

SANE
Contact Number 0300 304 7000
Available 4pm to 10pm 365 days a year
Offers emotional support and guidance for people affected from mental illness for both the sufferer and their family, friends and carers.

LGBT
Contact Number 0800 0119 100
Available every day 10am - 10pm
A support line to help people with mental health concerns, questioning their gender identity of coming out with their sexuality. Support for victims of hate crimes.

Rethink Mental Illness
Contact Number 0808 801 0525
Available Monday - Friday 9.30am to 4pm
Offer support and advice for people living with a mental illness

PAPYRUS
Contact Number 0800 068 4141
Available 9am - midnight 365 days a year
An organisation to help prevent the under 35s with suicidal intentions carrying them out.

BEAT
Contact Number 0808 801 0677
Available Monday - Friday Midday to 8pm, weekends and bank holidays 4pm -8pm
For anyone dealing with any type of eating disorder that needs support and advice

Barnardo's
Contact Number 0800 008 7005
A charity to support children who have been abused and give them support to feel safe again

ARCH (Abortion Recovery Care and Helpline)
Contact Number 0345 603 8501
Available Monday - Friday 9am to 5pm and 7pm to 10pm
Available to women, men and families for support

The Miscarriage Association
Contact number 01924 200799
Available Monday to Friday 9am to 4pm
For help and support and advice for those who have experienced miscarriage

Pandas Foundation
Contact Number 0808 1961 776
For people whose partners are suffering from pre or post natal depression

Fertility Network
Contact Number 01424 732361 or 0121 323 5025
For people affected by fertility issues

National Gambling Helpline
Contact Number 0808 8020 133
Available 24 hours a day 7 days a week
A helpline to assist when gambling has become out of control

MacMillian Support Line
Contact Number 0808 808 00 00
Available 7 days a week 8am - 8pm
For advice and support with all aspects of cancer

The Stress Management Society
Contact number 020 3142 8650
Available Monday to Friday 8.30am - 5.30pm
For individuals or companies who require support and advice concerning stress issues

Anxiety UK
Contact number 03444 775 775 or text 07537
Advice and support for people experiencing anxiety.

Chapter 11
Thank you

There are so many people I would like to thank but to all my family and friends who have put up with me constantly talking about this book and for all their shared love and support. I thank you all.

Thank you to Trish and Kevin for being there for me during my darkest hours. I cannot thank you enough for the support you gave me. I will always appreciate what you did for me.

I would like to individually thank Nicole and Gabby, two amazing people who I am so lucky to know. I thank you for your constant support and enthusiasm to help me finally complete this book.

I would also like to thank my masseuse, Jemma at Temple Therapies in Buckinghamshire, (jemmatemple@hotmail.com) for making all my tension vanish and make me feel wonderful and full of life every time I visit her.

I want to thank my wife, Helen, for her unconditional support and patience whilst I have spent hours hidden away writing this book.

Many thanks to We Talk Print in Bedford, for the wonderful promotional flyers for this book.

Most importantly, the biggest thank you goes to you for reading my book. I have put my heart and soul into this and I really believe if you have been open minded and not harshly judgemental on yourself you will greatly improve your wellbeing with your experiences of depression.

Please remember from negative feelings of low self esteem and feeling worthless, to frightful dark episodes that depression can take you to, believe in yourself. Support and help can always be found.

Be patient and positive and believe in yourself. Whichever method you choose be it via your GP, medication, counselling, support groups, alternative therapies as long as it brings you happiness and confidence again, it is a great choice.

The End

May all my family and friends, especially my sons Harrison and Alfie, know I love them all so very much and always will.

RIP
Dad, Mum and Michele xxx

I love you and think of you and miss you all everyday. You have made me turn my life into a positive one as you made me realise we only have one life.

SO LIVE IT AND LOVE IT

Printed in Great Britain
by Amazon

39539921R00066